MANAGERIAL
LEADERSHIP

Other books in The McGraw-Hill Executive MBA Series:

SALES MANAGEMENT
by Robert J. Calvin

CORPORATE STRATEGY
by John Colley, Jaqueline Doyle,
and Robert Hardie

FINANCE AND ACCOUNTING FOR NONFINANCIAL MANAGERS
by Samuel C. Weaver and J. Fred Weston

MERGERS AND ACQUISITIONS
by J. Fred Weston and Samuel C. Weaver

MANAGERIAL LEADERSHIP

THE McGRAW-HILL EXECUTIVE MBA SERIES

PETER A. TOPPING, PH.D.
Goizueta Business School
Emory University

Boston, Massachusetts   Burr Ridge, Illinois
Dubuque, Iowa   Madison, Wisconsin   New York, New York
San Francisco, California   St. Louis, Missouri

Library of Congress Cataloging-in-Publication Data

Topping, Peter (Peter A.)
    Managerial leadership/Peter Topping.
      p. cm.
    1. Leadership   2. Management. I. Title.
    ISBN 0-07-137523-6

    HD57.7 .T67 2001
    658.4—dc21   2001044865
                                          CIP

McGraw-Hill

A Division of The McGraw·Hill Companies

   3 4 5 6 7 8 9 BKM BKM   0 9 8 7 6 5

ISBN 0-07-137523-6
ISBN 0-07-145094-7-Paper

McGraw-Hill books are available at special quantity discounts to use as premiums and sales promotions, or for use in corporate training programs. For more information, please write to the Director of Special Sales, Professional Publishing, McGraw-Hill, Two Penn Plaza, New York, NY 10121-2298. Or contact your local bookstore.

*To my children and step-children:
Lindsay, Alex, Jason, Andrew, and
Carson, for their support and all
they have taught me about myself
and human behavior; and most
especially to my wife, Therese, for
her incredible love, encouragement,
and wisdom.*

CONTENTS

PREFACE

I remember talking in 1995 with Bob Staton, CEO of Colonial Life & Accident Insurance Company, a division of UNUM, about the lack of leadership throughout the company. Colonial was one of the few large, homegrown companies in Columbia, South Carolina, when it was acquired by UNUM, the Maine-based disability insurance company. At first, there was little evidence of the takeover, as UNUM kept its distance from the folks at Colonial. But as inevitably happens, eventually the parent company became more and more engaged with the day-to-day activities of its acquisition —particularly when the return on the investment began to erode. Colonial had been a successful independent company throughout the 1970s and 1980s, but its margins got tighter and top-line growth became increasingly more difficult as the insurance world began to change. The pressure was mounting for Colonial to produce better financial results. As a result, Staton and the senior management team were looking inward, as well as outward, for possible solutions.

One of the outcomes of their search was the idea to create a new leadership development program for all the managers in the company. I was interviewing Staton as part of the field research to design the program. During the conversation, he was quite clear in expressing his concern that Colonial had too many managers and not enough leaders. It was too much for me to resist asking him what the difference was—between a manager and a leader. Staton's response was similar to what I've heard many times from senior-level executives both before and since this conversation. "Managers," he said, "wait to be told what to do," while leaders "take initiative, figure out what has to be done, and then do it."

Whatever happened to the value of sound management? It seems to have become a pariah in the business world. The cry for getting rid of "managers" and replacing them with "leaders" is loud and clear. Given the popularity of Drucker's seminal work, *The Practice of Management*, in the 1950s, how far have we fallen? Do we really need to rid organizations of managers entirely?

Dick Blackburn, a former colleague of mine at the University of North Carolina, used the expression "managerial leadership"over 15 years ago in referring to the challenges midlevel managers face inside complex organizations. That expression has durably stuck in my memory despite the desperate fight for space for such things. Recently, it has become increasingly clear to me why it stuck. I have heard so many executives like Bob Staton lament the lack of leadership within their companies at the same time as I have heard scores of managers lament the ever-increasing amount of work they are asked to execute. Is this a contradiction in terms or just an illustration of the tension between getting things done and developing people?

The fact is that we still clearly have a need for good managers —people who are able to effectively plan, organize, direct and control. We also have a great need for leaders inside organizations—people who inspire, motivate, and develop others. And we need leaders at all levels in our organization, not just at the top. The old adage that we manage things and lead people applies here, albeit with a slight revision—the need is to successfully manage projects and activities while simultaneously leading people effectively.

With all deference to Professor Blackburn, *Managerial Leadership* was selected as the title for this book, as it best describes the leadership issues organizations face today. While it can be argued that senior executives need to manage also, certainly at or below the general manager level it is imperative that organizations have people who are capable as both managers and leaders. This presents a huge individual challenge, as the skill sets are quite different between the two. Typically, the high potentials have shown managerial competence, but it is the leadership piece that will successfully propel them on to the next level. It also presents a huge organizational challenge. Most companies have learned how to develop the management piece (the task side) among the midlevel employees but struggle mightily in developing the leadership component. That used to be sufficient but it isn't any longer. To borrow from Bob Staton's commentary, the leadership vacuum inside the organization is a serious detriment to performance.

The focus of this book is on the leadership side of managerial leadership. Without diminishing the importance of good management, the critical need today is to enhance managers' leadership behaviors (especially those with the lowercase "l," not the leadership challenges at the top of the organization but rather those in the middle of the action). I have written this book with the same learning objectives and approach as the leadership development programs that I design and conduct. Having been at this business for more than 15 years, I have seen it work.

But so much depends upon the individual's motivation for learning and change. Enhancing leadership practices is a highly personal endeavor. Given how difficult it is to unlearn bad habits, it takes a huge amount of emotional energy to change leadership behaviors. And, unfortunately, there is no one right answer or one model that works for everyone and applies to every situation. That is why I do not propose a specific approach or a single framework. My premise is that you need to build your own leadership model —one that works best for you—that takes into account your capabilities and leadership style, as well as the organizational environment and dynamics of your followers.

Can anyone teach you to be a better leader? It is a frequently asked question and one I understand well. (Given my role as an executive educator, perhaps my answer will surprise you.) It reminds me of a psychology course I took in the early 1970s. Professor John Carroll was teaching the class. I never understood how such an internationally renowned psychometrician wound up teaching a group of ignorant undergraduates. Most of his lectures not only went over our heads, but they were in a completely different dimension of time and space. However, one lecture actually got through to me. Dr. Carroll was debating the nature versus nurture question with himself (as he was the only one in the room capable of attempting such a debate), and he asserted that it was a "so-what" question. It didn't matter how much of human behavior was dictated by genetics versus socialization (this was before the breakthroughs in genetic engineering). Dr. Carroll believed that even if socialization accounted for only 10 percent of human behavior, so what? Since we couldn't do anything about the nature part, the only issue of consequence was to concentrate on the proportion related to nurture.

In making the application to leadership, we ask how much is inherent to the individual versus how much can be developed. Borrowing from Professor Carroll, it doesn't really matter. Even if teaching can only enhance 10 percent of your leadership effectiveness, it's worth the attention. Think about it. In any organization, to what extent are the managers operating at their full capabilities—

certainly not at 100 percent of their potential. If we can teach them how to be more effective leaders, even very modest improvements in each person can reap big rewards for the entire organization. So can leadership be taught? Not in the way we can teach mathematics or discounted cashflow, but a heightened understanding of how leadership behaviors affect others and impact performance can help anyone enhance his or her effectiveness.

And isn't any gain in this area worth the effort? Virtually all of today's leadership gurus agree that what distinguishes successful managers and executives from the masses are their leadership capabilities. Having worked with literally hundreds of business people over the past two decades, across diverse industries and national boundaries, I know the light of enlightenment can be lit. With enlightenment, commitment, and a willingness to work hard on behavior change, you can develop yourself into a more effective leader. The return on that investment can be exceptionally high. If this book helps you on that journey, then I will be very pleased—for both of us!

ACKNOWLEDGMENTS

Many people played important roles in helping me write this book. Certainly, I owe a great deal of thanks to all the managers and executives who have generously shared their wisdom with me over these past 20 years.

On a more personal note, two of my colleagues at Goizueta Business School, Professors Rick Gilkey and Jagdish Sheth, encouraged my efforts and offered sage advice. My associates on the executive education staff provided a lot of support and enabled me to dedicate the time required to complete the book. I also wish to thank Irene McMorland for her efforts as my research assistant.

Kelli Christiansen has been a very patient and supportive editor. I am also appreciative of my brother Stephen, himself an accomplished editor and publisher, for giving me the benefit of his keen insight and perspective about writing. And I am especially grateful to my wife, Therese, from whom I have learned a great deal these past two years about leadership, human behavior, and the nuances of the profession of psychiatry.

PART ONE

LEADING CHANGE AS A MANAGER; MANAGING CHANGE AS A LEADER

CHAPTER 1

Looking Out, Before Looking In

"To business that we love we rise betime,
And go to't with delight."
— Marc Antony, *Antony and Cleopatra*
William Shakespeare

People don't work in vacuums, and so leadership issues must be viewed within a context. For a crude but effective illustration, watch the movies *Patton* and *Gandhi*. Granted, especially as depicted in the movies, these men are complex, larger-than-life people, but one leadership lesson is relevant at any level. General Patton had a leadership style quite different from Mahatma Gandhi's—yet both men were (arguably) highly effective in their times. Could you see them switching places and still being effective? Clearly, Gandhi would not have been a very successful general of the Third Army during World War II, nor would Patton have been able to lead a nonviolent social revolution in British-controlled India.

As you begin analyzing your leadership effectiveness, start by looking at your environment before you examine your internal leadership style. The term *situational leadership* has taken on a specific reference to a model proposed by Ken Blanchard. However, in a more generic sense, the concept of situational leadership suggests that one size does not fit all. Only by reviewing the situation you are in—incorporating the work environment, followers, and industry challenges—can you best determine the leadership behaviors that would make you the most effective.

Leadership theory evolved in this direction over the course of the twentieth century. Leadership scholars moved from the "great man theory" (which implied that leaders were born, not made) in the early 1900s to a more comprehensive view of leadership that took into account the interactions between the task, the leader, and relationships with followers. Add to this the impact of the sociocultural dynamics at work within the organization and within the business environment before determining which leadership style(s) fits best. It is commonly thought today that enlightened leaders are participative, encouraging, and focused on the development of their people. However, there may well be circumstances where that set of leadership practices would not be the most appropriate. Think, for example, of a company in crisis where there is an urgent need for change and a strong organizational culture in place that resists change. Add to the mix a work force that is experienced, cynical, and lacking accountability. Certainly, to be effective in this situation, at least in the short term, you would need to employ a more command-and-control leadership style than a developmental one.

It seems simple enough, but it's not. One of the lessons I have learned over the years is that changing your leadership practices to adapt to differing situations is extraordinarily difficult. George Patton couldn't do it. As the inner workings of the army became more visible with increased media coverage, his bullying tactics and crude behaviors were no longer appropriate. He could not adapt to this different environment. A similar analysis has been applied to the problems that Bobby Knight experienced as the men's basketball coach at Indiana University. Changes in society's view of college athletics, and changes in the athletes themselves, had a profound influence on his ability to succeed.

Yet while behavioral change is challenging, you cannot possibly get there if you are not aware that such a change is warranted in the first place. Thus, it is in your best interest to spend some time analyzing your situation before taking a good, hard look at yourself. Your goal should be to focus more on aligning your leadership behaviors with the demands of your environment, rather than trying to force the environment to adjust to your set style. You do not need to spend months or even weeks on this external analysis, but you should go about it systematically and as objectively as possible.

UNDERSTANDING YOUR FOLLOWERS

Another critical part of your external analysis is to consider the dynamics of the people you will be leading. After all, there is no leadership without followers. Their capabilities, aspirations, personalities, and interactions with each other have direct bearing on how they need to be led. One department I took over had eight employees—most of whom had been working together in that same department for more than five years. My predecessor had been head of this unit for about 15 years and had exhibited a high need for control in the way he managed the office. I am most comfortable operating as a visionary leader—setting the big picture, being (I hope) inspiring, and empowering the staff to act without direct supervision. I hate being micromanaged and therefore do not prefer to exercise tight control over others. It did not take me terribly long to realize that operating in my preferred style in that department was not going to work. The employees had become too accustomed to how the unit had been operating and could not adjust to a significantly different approach. The dilemma I faced was how to address the competing interests of the staff's needs to be told what to do and my strong desire not to have to supervise that closely. In that situation, it took some time, but I was eventually able to find a place of balance—both sides adjusting to enable effective performance. It required a few personnel changes and, most importantly, my acknowledging that I needed to adapt to my new staff as much as they needed to adapt to their new director.

In trying to better understand your followers, consider the following characteristics of the individuals and the group as a whole:

- Experience in the industry
- Experience in the organization
- The way they were managed in the past
- The impact of the "demographic" diversity in the group (e.g., age, gender, race, and ethnicity)
- The influence of the "psychographic" diversity in the group (e.g., lifestyles, personality traits, and family dynamics)
- Major recent life experiences

The time invested in understanding the influence of these factors among your associates will be well worth it as you consider your leadership options.

One of the most frustrating issues for managerial leaders is the seemingly broad chasm between the different generations in today's work force. It's not as if generational differences didn't exist before, but there appears to be much more definition between the groups than I can remember. In 1999, Randstad North America, a subsidiary of Randstad Holding nv of The Netherlands, commissioned Roper Starch Worldwide to conduct a comprehensive study of the differences among the generations in the work force. As a company that focuses on staffing and employment, Randstad NA was seeking more clarity on work force dynamics to help it better serve its customers. The published Roper Starch report, entitled *Employee Review: Insights into Workforce Attitudes*, contains some very interesting findings. The report defines four adult generations that comprise the twenty-first-century work force:

- *Matures* (35 million people, ages 55–69)
- *Baby Boomers* (76 million, 37–55)
- *GenXers* (60 million, 21–36)
- *GenYers* (sometimes referred to as "Generation D"—the digital generation—representing 74 million people born after 1980)

There is a good deal of variance within the generations, and so it is dangerous to make broad-scale generalizations across these age groups. But there is also a good bit of consistency within each group that enables us to better appreciate the leadership implications of managing today's work force.

For example, the Matures generation is connected to World War II and all the social change resulting from the post-Depression economic recovery spurred by the war. As they became adults, Matures experienced the heat of the cold war. They reflect more of the "rags-to-riches" phenomenon as a result of their growing up in a very depressed economy compared with the prosperity that followed World War II. As the Roper Report writes:

Matures tend to buy into the status quo and often seem to possess a traditional sense of dedication to their company and job.

The Baby Boomer generation, with births between the years 1946 and 1964, grew up in the midst of significant social unrest in the United States. One of the key ways that the Baby Boomers differ from the Matures is that the Baby Boomers were activists in creating social change—particularly with regard to the Vietnam War and the civil rights movement. The sheer numbers of Baby Boomers had a great impact on the nation and on U.S. views on race, gender, and youth. With their skepticism about authority and desire for personal freedom, Baby Boomers "helped to revolutionize the workplace by pushing for casual work environments, flexible schedules, and the opportunity to work from home."

Those born between 1965 and 1980 fall under Generation X. Their formative years took place during a time of dramatic changes in corporate America—major downsizings and layoffs with formerly imperturbable *Fortune* 100 companies (IBM, General Motors, AT&T, for example), and the rise in financial wealth brought on by junk bonds and Wall Street wizardry. GenXers, as they are called, thus have a lot less loyalty to their employing organization and a greater interest in luxury and the finer things in life. They put a premium on individuality and entrepreneurship.

The youngest generation in the work force, Generation Y, has not yet experienced a prolonged downturn in the economy. Born after 1980, GenYers are typically optimistic and place a lot of faith in technology. They are truly the multimedia generation, seeking great amounts of stimulation. Yet, according to RoperStarch, this generation can best be described as "trailblazing traditionalists" where their "enthusiasm for the future is built on a solid foundation of religion, family and a sound work ethic." In this context, GenYers are more akin to their grandparents (the parents of Baby Boomers) than they are to the Boomers themselves.

The ramifications of these generational differences in the work place are summarized in Table 1.1. For example, the views on employment expectations vary from the "cradle-to-grave" of Matures to "on my own terms" for Baby Boomers and "entrepre-

T a b l e   1.1

Generational mindsets.

	Working-Age Matures	Baby Boomers	GenXers GenYers
Employment Expectations	Cradle-to-grave	On my terms	Entrepreneurial
The "Office"	Work at my desk	Work at home	Work "virtually" anywhere
Relationship between Work & Leisure	Purpose of leisure is to recharge batteries for work	Work now so you can play later	Never the twain shall meet
The Home	Multigenerational	Nuclear family	Back in the nest with Mom and Dad
Fun	Saturday night "out"	Staying "in"	Surfing the "Web" from anywhere
Financial Focus	Save for a rainy day	Indulge	Invest in an IPO
Icons	Lee Iococca	Ben & Jerry	Jeff Bezos
Formative Years Indentity	Date and Mate romantics	Flower children	Hip hoppers
Millennial Mindset	Batten down the hatches	Live for today	Prepare for the best

neurial" for GenXers/GenYers. Yes, it is obvious that you motivate a 58-year-old manager differently from how you motivate a 32-year-old. What may not be obvious are the techniques you should use based upon the differences between the generations. Where the 40-year-old is looking for some ability to control the environment and work on his or her own terms, the 30-year-old will respond well to opportunities to expand his or her skills and knowledge and to work with start-up activities inside the company.

We know the world and see others through our own inner reality. To be truly effective in understanding how to best lead others, you need to see the world through their reality, not your own. The classic expression that you can't understand someone until you walk in his shoes addresses the key point. You don't need to literally walk in their shoes, but you must try to understand your followers by connecting with their perspectives on life and work. When you catch yourself thinking, "I don't understand how they can act that way," you will know that you are on the right path. Instead of throwing up your hands in disgust, try to figure out how they perceive the situation to enable you to better understand their behaviors. The best way to learn how others see things is to ask open-ended questions that would have your associates describe their perceptions in some detail. By acknowledging that you view the world differently, you will begin to help your followers recognize that there are generational variances that affect the way you work together. As with people who speak different languages, the fact that both parties want to communicate effectively is 80 percent of the battle. Learn to talk about the ways your perceptions vary and you will find ways to more effectively communicate.

EXAMPLES OF THE BEST CURRENT THINKING ON LEADERSHIP

The next time you have the chance to conduct an online search for articles and publications, type in *leadership* as the keyword and see the results. You will get thousands of citations covering every angle imaginable—from "Leadership Lessons from Attilla the Hun" to Red Auerbach's leadership philosophy from his days coaching the Boston Celtics. New books on leadership are published every month, with the promise of a fresh look or revolutionary perspective. The messages are all quite similar, however, and do not vary much from decade to decade. So why do we continue to buy the books? If so many smart people have been studying leadership for all these years, why don't we have the answer?

The answer, of course, is that there is no answer—at least no one right answer. But we all want *the answer*, so we keep looking for it. Every now and then, a new approach to leadership will come out that captures a lot of attention. Stephen Covey's *Seven Habits of Highly Effective People* was one such example, as was Ken Blanchard's *The One Minute Manager*.

What captures our attention isn't new information, but rather the way the information is presented—the framework the author uses to describe leadership principles. John Kotter and Warren Bennis are two examples of leadership writers who presented new models that were well received when first published. Scholars such as Kotter and Bennis reflected the *best current thinking* on leadership of the times. They advanced our awareness and presented their views in ways that effectively resonated with large numbers of people.

Today's best current thinkers on leadership include James Kouzes and Barry Posner (*The Leadership Challenge*) and Daniel Goleman (*Emotional Intelligence*). A brief look at their models will help illustrate some of the important elements that define how organizations view leadership effectiveness at the onset of the twenty-first century.

The Kouzes and Posner model, first described in *The Leadership Challenge*, was based upon their research into the leadership practices of "effective managers." They collected data from several thousand people, at various levels in organizations, who had been identified as being successful in the way they led others. In determining what practices and behaviors were common among those effective managerial leaders, Kouzes and Posner zeroed in on five competencies:

- Challenging the process
- Inspiring a shared vision
- Enabling others to act
- Modeling the way
- Encouraging the heart

With some further definition of each of those five principal leadership practices, Kouzes and Posner developed a 360° feedback instrument designed to assess an individual's effectiveness as perceived by his or her peers, subordinates, and supervisor(s). The Leadership Practices Inventory has become a widely used tool for taking a relatively high-level view of the consistency of perceptions across these levels about an individual manager. Their model incorporates principles that have been associated with leadership for quite some time, but the way the practices are pieced together has attracted a following.

One of the major themes in their work is the importance of being positive and optimistic as a managerial leader. Kouzes and

Posner utilized the concept of a "personal best" leadership experience in collecting their data. In that context, leading via encouragement, celebration, the envisioning of an uplifting future, and positive recognition were found to be most powerful.

Optimism in the face of failure is one of the specific practices identified in their work. What a tremendous challenge this is for a managerial leader. You may be very frustrated with your organization, and learned the hard way to be cynical about all the new and improved initiatives or restructurings, but you cannot let that adversely affect your ability to keep your people positive.

I remember working with a plant manager—let's call him Sam—whose company was going through a downsizing in its manufacturing operations. Rumors were abundant, as the grapevine is always lightning fast. Sam's plant was actually in good shape and wasn't one of the facilities targeted for shutdown. His people didn't know that, however. Sam was a member of the company's task force that was charged with recommending the cutbacks. On one particular day, Sam had arrived at his plant early in the morning for an all-day meeting of the task force. He had been up most of the night due to some difficulties at home, and so he was tired, upset, and distracted as he entered the plant. As Sam walked down the hallway toward the meeting room, an associate of Sam's—Carla—was heading in the opposite direction. Despite the fact that Carla was a few levels below Sam on the organizational chart, they certainly knew each other. Naturally, Carla said hello to Sam as they passed each other in the hallway, but he didn't even notice her. Sam was so preoccupied with his own distress that he walked right by Carla without saying a word. Thirty minutes later, being very upset, Carla went to the office of the director of human resources at the plant. She was convinced that her name was at the top of the list to be let go since, as she reported to the HR director, "he didn't even have the guts to look me in the eye."

It's not fair to expect Sam to be cheerful and smiling all the time. All of us are entitled to have a bad day, but we must be aware of the impact of our attitudes on others when we are in leadership positions. Kouzes and Posner identified this as a key managerial leadership issue—keeping yourself positive, despite the difficult circumstances around you, as a way of motivating others to perform.

Focusing on encouraging the heart has made a significant impact at a Lockheed Martin business unit, according to Leonard Hicks. As a director in the unit, Leonard and his colleagues are using the Kouzes and Posner framework to serve as their leadership model, to the extent that Leonard has spent considerable time with Barry Posner at the University of Santa Clara in California. During a rendition of Lockheed's Strategic Leadership Development Program, which I direct through my work at Emory University (in Georgia), Leonard talked about their efforts. He said that the value of using the leadership practices framework was in the consistency it instilled across the managers in the business unit. They were all focused on the same leadership behaviors and were enthusiastic in the way in which they were progressing. This demonstrates once again that it is not the model that counts per se, but the execution of the leadership model that makes the difference.

Daniel Goleman's leadership model was first presented in his book *Emotional Intelligence*. It provides a psychological perspective on human behavior and the concepts surrounding intelligence that is fairly theoretical and difficult for a layperson to understand. However, in 1998 Goleman published a *Harvard Business Review* article that distilled the theory into a more applied view of leadership behaviors based on emotional intelligence. "What Makes a Leader" spoke of the differences between intellect, technical ability, and emotional maturity as they apply to organizational behavior. Goleman's basic premise is that our standard measures of intelligence, while accurate, are not valid measures of success in life. He postulates that other factors are much more highly correlated with success—factors that Goleman defined as "emotional intelligence" (EQ). In its application to leadership, an individual's EQ has more relevance than IQ in determining effectiveness, according to Goleman. The five components of EQ are:

- Self-awareness
- Self-regulation
- Motivation
- Empathy
- Social skills

There isn't a whole lot new in the theory once you examine the elements that compose these five components. They include:

- Self-confidence, realistic self-assessment, healthy self-deprecation (self-awareness)
- Trustworthiness, integrity, ability to effectively deal with ambiguity (self-regulation)
- Ability to recruit and retain talent, drive for achievement, openness to change (motivation)
- Cross-cultural awareness, ability to relate well to customers and colleagues (empathy)
- Persuasiveness, ability to build and lead teams (social skills)

None of these elements differs significantly from leadership models proposed over the past 30 years, but the way Goleman presents these principles is resonating in organizations today. Perhaps it is the message that you don't have to be the smartest to be an effective leader. Rather, emotional maturity and credibility play more important roles in how well you provide leadership inside an organization. A key question is can EQ be developed, or is it another frustrating example of the nature-nurture debate? If you answer that question by counting how many seminars are held each year on emotional intelligence in the workplace, you would assume that EQ can definitely be developed. I have my doubts, however. Certainly, portions of the EQ elements can be enhanced through developmental activities. The components that incorporate empathy and social skills would be among them. For example, I have personally taught many sessions to executives on cross-cultural awareness, relationship marketing, and team building. Through those experiences, I have a good bit of anecdotal evidence that skills can be sharpened and effectiveness enhanced.

The elements within self-regulation and motivation are harder for me to see as being easily developed in managers. So much of leadership revolves around values—your values juxtaposed with those of your followers and your organization—and I do not believe that values can be taught to adults. This in no way prevents us from trying to develop leadership in managers. It simply assists in aiming—the targets to shoot for are those areas in which behavior change can occur through developmental activities.

I do not give up on the values piece, despite my comments on the implausibility of teaching values to adults. It is certainly appropriate to raise the issues of how values and leadership practices interact. I prefer to view these types of issues along a continuum, as opposed to categorizing people in discrete boxes. For example, if we look at a continuum for ethical behavior, we would have *extremely unethical* at one end and *extremely ethical* at the other. Let's say for argument's sake that we could agree on a definition of ethical behavior. Obviously most people would fall somewhere toward the middle to upper middle end of the continuum. Through serious learning activities, it would be possible to help someone move along the continuum toward a higher level of ethical behavior, even if only incrementally. This might be particularly evident in certain situations where a pending decision falls within a rather gray area. By making you more aware of the ethical dilemmas people face in business every day, providing a framework for your decision making process, and raising your awareness of acting ethically even under difficult circumstances, I believe your decision making in these ambiguous circumstances can be influenced toward more ethical behavior. In this way, values can be influenced through developmental activities. But to be so influenced, the individual would need to be at a certain ethical level already.

In the leadership development business, it is essential to gain an appreciation of the underlying values structure of the individual(s) in question. Those at the tail end, whose value systems have not been fully developed (for whatever reasons), are not truly capable of learning leadership. They may certainly demonstrate some positive leadership characteristics, but so much of being a strong managerial leader is connected with the values of openness, integrity, trustworthiness, respect for others, and honesty that people lacking these qualities can never be effective leaders.

CONFIDENCE

The predominant leadership philosophy in the early part of my career emphasized the heroic approach that utilized the metaphor of the proverbial hero (masculine gender always assumed) riding in on his white horse to solve all problems and defeat the enemy. The heroic leader was someone who had all the answers. To be successful, the rest of the organization just needed to follow. Obviously, to be perceived as this type of leader, you had to demonstrate complete command and control. Showing any signs of uncertainty or need for help from others communicated weakness. Lee Iacocca was an appropriate icon of the heroic leader—coming in to Chrysler to save the company from certain collapse. The heroic leader approach is still alive today, but the effectiveness of this style has been very much in question over the past few years. *Fortune* magazine ran a 1995 cover story on the "new post heroic leadership" in corporate America. The article stressed that organizations needed leaders who were more empowering than commanding, The post heroic leader would acknowledge not having all the answers but would motivate and inspire subordinates to find the right answers by asking the right questions and getting everyone engaged in the activity.

Jim Collins (coauthor in 1994 of *Built to Last* with Jerry Porras) published an article in the January 2001 *Harvard Business Review* that further argues against the efficacy of heroic leadership. In his research, Collins found that lasting success (as measured by sustained financial performance dramatically above industry averages) was most directly attributable to humility at the top—what he classified as Level 5 leadership. Collins's theoretical approach is similar to Kohlberg's five stages of moral development, where Level 5 is descriptive of the most highly advanced and sophisticated individuals. Following Kohlberg's model, this is not achievable by most people. Only a few are capable of functioning at the highest level. And, according to Collins, it is the key point of differentiation in comparing sustained excellence with short-lived success in corporate performance—even more so than technological innovation and brand equity. That's a striking statement and contrary to the (still) prevailing view that leadership at the CEO level should be more heroic than humble.

How fine is the line between arrogance and self-confidence? As with many other phenomena, I don't see these as two distinct buckets where you are clearly in either one or the other. It seems more an issue of "shades of gray" than black and white. Most of us fall somewhere in between the extreme behaviors of pure arrogance and total insecurity. It is hard to imagine that someone with a complete lack of self-confidence could be an effective leader at any point in time. Decisions have to be made, and that requires confidence. Followers, in order to be truly motivated to follow, need to have some confidence in the ability of their leader. Part of that feeling of confidence in their leader comes from the leader's confidence in himself or herself. Thinking back over the past three decades of working with leaders at all levels in organizations, I cannot recall a time when self-confidence wasn't an important quality in effective leadership. There was a reason that Jack Welch used the slogan "Speed, Simplicity and Self-Confidence" when describing his vision for General Electric back in the nineties.

While the same timelessness applies to the relationship between arrogance and leadership, it is magnified as we enter the twenty-first century. Defined by Webster's *Intercollegiate Dictionary* as "offensively exaggerating one's own importance," the term *arrogant* characterizes leaders of yesterday and today—there has never been an era lacking in arrogant leaders. Here it is important to distinguish between a command-and-control leadership style and the manifestation of narcissism—one is a behavioral style and the other reflects a personality disorder. You can operate with an autocratic approach to managing others and have humility. Typically, someone who uses this style comes out of an environment where the command-and-control model was predominant. We parent our children following the way we were parented. In that same context, we tend to lead people in organizations the way we have been led.

This is different from arrogance, which is a personality trait, not a leadership style. They may look alike, however. Arrogant leaders are naturally authoritative. They believe they have all the answers and make no mistakes. The key distinction between the autocratic style and arrogance centers on whose needs are being met—the leader's or the organization's. Arrogant people put their needs above all else. Effective leaders put the organization's needs (as well as the needs of their followers) above their own. Arrogance will eventually erode a leader's effectiveness. This appears to be truer today than at any time over the past 30 years. Given the incredible complexities of business, the demand for very sophisticated interpersonal skills in highly networked organizations, and the need to develop people to their fullest, the self-serving righteousness of narcissistic leaders is completely out of place. I'm not so naïve as to believe it doesn't exist in today's executive suites, but I am convinced that high levels of arrogance are much more likely to lead to career derailment and failure than ever before.

It is critical that you be aware of your level of self-confidence. There are significant implications regarding your leadership behaviors on where you fall on the continuum from insecurity to self-confidence to arrogance. Of course, highly arrogant individuals are incapable of realistic self-assessment. But you can be leaning in the direction of arrogance and still have enough introspection to acknowledge it—and, the hope is, to alter it. Reflect on whose needs come first. Are your subordinates there to serve you, or are you there to serve them and your organization? Perhaps imagining a seesaw would help illustrate this point. When the balance is such that the individual on the other side has his or her needs met, you rise up. Make sure that you keep that thought in your frontal lobe as you make decisions. The concept of servant leadership (most notably written about by Gardner) is hinged on this very important fulcrum. Help yourself to develop the confidence to inspire others and enable you to take the actions you know you must take. Keep yourself from slipping into arrogance, either as a cover for your insecurity or as a means for getting what you want. As a managerial leader, you will go further when you concentrate on serving others rather than on serving yourself.

SELF-AWARENESS

In Abraham Maslow's seminal work on the hierarchy of needs, self-actualization represented the top of the pyramid (Table 1.2). According to his theory, the drive to understand self was the highest level of satisfying human needs and could only be met when other, more primitive drives were satisfied first. In the context of leadership, the ability to truly understand one's self is also at the pinnacle. This is easy to say and extraordinarily complicated to do. Short of prolonged psychotherapy, true self-awareness is difficult

T a b l e   1.2

Maslow's hierachy of needs.

Level	Type of Need	Examples
1	Physiology	Thirst, sex, hunger
2	Safety	Security, stability, protection
3	Love and belongingness	To escape loneliness, love and be loved, and gain a sense of belonging
4	Esteem	Self-respect, the respect of others
5	Self-actualization	To fulfill one's potentialities

to achieve. While I believe in the power of psychotherapy, I am not advocating it for everyone. The issue becomes, how can you go about achieving a realistic self-assessment of your leadership strengths and weaknesses?

It starts with your desire to do so—coupled with the ability to be introspective. Some people are naturals at this. They have the capacity to be self-critical for the purpose of understanding and positive growth. However, like most people I know, I have a hard time with this. My defense mechanisms are too well established, so I am able to rationalize most of my problems as being due to external forces. Deeply rooted insecurities take over and make it extremely difficult to take an intensive, candid look in the mirror. Take it as a basic human trait that we are instinctively closed to honest self-reflection but that we can overcome our instincts. In fact, it is a sign of significant maturity when you are able to work through your defenses to candidly reflect on your capabilities and shortcomings. From this self-understanding, you will best be able to leverage your talents and know when to ask for help in overcoming deficiencies. The people who work with you are able to see what you are good at doing and where you struggle. If you lack that insight, and relentlessly work in your areas of weakness, you lose credibility. And without credibility, a leader has no legs to stand on.

On the other hand, a leader's ability to leverage his or her strengths is inspirational to others, especially when coupled with an open acknowledgment of areas of deficiency. In this era of post-heroic leadership, rather than being a sign of weakness to admit to one's shortcomings, it is a sign of strength of character. There are no absolutes in business, so why assume that there are any absolutes for leading in a business? Nobody expects you to have all the answers. They just hope you know the questions and can then lead them in helping to find the answers.

SELF-ASSESSMENT TOOLS

A variety of tools are available to help promote self-awareness in the context of leadership. One of the most powerful of these is 360° feedback. The term derives from a full-circle (360°) view of an individual's leadership behaviors as perceived by peers, subordinates, and supervisor(s). Many types of 360° instruments are on the market, ranging from superficial to highly complex measures of management and leadership practices (see Appendix B for sample profiles from a 360° feedback instrument). In an ideal world, this type of intervention would be unnecessary, as we would routinely know how others perceived us. The giving and receiving of feedback would be an everyday occurrence. But there is no ideal world of which I am aware. It is highly uncommon for communication inside organizations to be so open that perceptions are regularly exchanged. It is one of those fascinating human traits that we all want constant feedback to know how we are doing and yet we are all so reluctant to give it.

Many companies utilize 360° feedback as a part of their human resource development initiatives. If used wisely, it can strongly enhance leadership behaviors. If done poorly, the use of 360° feedback can backfire and cause significant damage within the company. I have seen both best and worst practices in the implementation of 360s. An illustration of a best practice is seen in an insurance company that built the 360° instrument rollout into a five-day leadership development program. A significant amount of training was provided both to the individuals who would receive the feedback and to all the feedback providers so that their input could be as meaningful as possible. The feedback recipients were given a good deal of time, with coaching, to analyze the information they received. Then, these same managers participated in a program that integrated the 360° competencies into the course content. In this way, the managers could focus on building their capabilities in a supportive classroom environment. As a pretest-posttest measurement, the managers were given the opportunity to get another round of 360° feedback six to eight months later in order to assess their progress. In all ways, the use of the 360° instrument was viewed as a developmental tool, not an evaluative performance appraisal device.

Which brings me to a worst-practice example—a major corporation that paid seven figures for a "customized" 360° instrument from a major private consulting firm. The company spent all its resources on the instrument and did not build a developmental experience around the feedback. Training to feedback providers was haphazardly done, so there was a minimal amount of consistency in the data collected. And the profiles were used for performance reviews rather than as developmental tools. Therefore, the recipients selected those feedback providers who would make them look good, not those who would give good constructive criticism. Most importantly, the company was not ready for 360° feedback because it had a culture that fostered covert communications and was highly political. The implementation was an unmitigated disaster and cost a number of people their reputations— and for a few, it resulted in their terminations. Fortunately, the company realized how bad the situation had become, and it stopped using the 360° instrument until it could find a way to do it more effectively. The sad part is that it will take quite some time before the people in that company will trust a feedback-based instrument again—and they need it the most!

There are a variety of other self-assessment instruments that can provide additional insight for understanding leadership behaviors and styles—all aimed at enhancing self-awareness. The Myers Briggs Type Indicator (MBTI) is probably the most widely used personality indicator. FIRO-B is another popular instrument that was often used by the Center for Creative Leadership. Among my favorites are the Birkman and the Learning Styles Inventory, each of which offers a unique perspective for self–assessment. It is important to take some care in selecting the instrument(s) that would add the most value for you in this process. Look for:

- A well-validated instrument—sufficiently tested and utilized
- A tool that measures factors important to you and your job responsibilities
- An instrument that is neither too superficial nor too complex to be useful

In high-quality leadership programs conducted by reputable institutions, it is common for participants to undergo an array of assessment instruments. In most of the programs that I have designed, we employ at least three tools, including the 360° feedback instrument. Each one provides unique information that can be helpful in the self-assessment process. But no tool is perfect. All these measurements are "slippery" at best in that they involve human behavior, perception, and highly intangible variables. Thus, the use of multiple instruments, coupled with the individual's introspective capabilities, enables the best opportunity for a comprehensive view of competency.

SUMMARY

The bad news is that there is no one right model for everyone to follow that guarantees you will become a more effective leader. The good news is that you can create your own model—one that fits your environment and organizational dynamics, accounts for the types of followers that you are leading, and plays upon your strengths and minimizes your deficiencies. There are a number of popular frameworks to pull from—most notably Daniel Goleman's work on emotional intelligence and the five exemplary leadership practices identified by Kouzes and Posner.

In building your own leadership model, leverage your talents. This requires you to take a good hard look at yourself in the mirror. Continuous, realistic self-assessment creates a solid platform from which you can launch your development plan—a path forward for self-improvement and growth. There are ample tools to assist you in this process—with 360° feedback at the core. But none of these steps will be effective without your having the desire to improve your leadership effectiveness. It all starts there—your commitment and perseverance for behavioral change. As *Star Wars'* Yoda proclaimed, "There is no try . . . there is only do or not do." Don't start down this path unless you really want to make the journey. If you do, you won't regret it!

QUESTIONS AND EXERCISES

- Write a brief description of the work force segments that are the most relevant for your organization. What are the key differences among the groups? What leadership style(s) are best aligned with each group?

- Pick your company's top three competitors and research their cultures. How are the companies different from your company and from each other? How do customers perceive the differences among all the firms? What does this analysis say about the current status of the industry? What major changes in competition might occur over the next three years that could significantly alter the industry?

- Create a leadership time line for yourself (beginning with the end of high school) that depicts important turning points in your development as a managerial leader. Think of where you have been and where you are today on the time line. What do you expect it to look like in five years? Ten years?

CHAPTER 2

The Forces of Change

"There is nothing more difficult to carry out,
nor more doubtful of success, nor more danger-
ous to handle, than to initiate a new order of
things."

— Machiavelli

There is nothing new about change. Machiavelli wrote about it centuries ago. The Old and New Testaments are full of stories about change. I cannot think of a period in business when "change" hasn't been an important concern. So why is it such a hot topic in boardrooms, executive suites, and management development programs today? Most managers describe the pace and scope of change as the key reasons. Change today is constant. There is no stopping it and there is no standing still. In this way, change is a relentlessly powerful force pounding on organizations.

I was taught a rather simple model for addressing corporate change when I was in graduate school. Being somewhat simple-minded, I liked the model (see Figure 2.1). First, you had to "unfreeze" from the current status quo, move through a short-term (orchestrated) transition period, and "refreeze" once you reached the desired state, where you would lock in the new status quo. Nice generic model. Unfortunately, it does not work today because there is no time to "refreeze." By the time you could get to the desired state, the world would have changed again, and so a new target would have to be set. This fundamental revision of a relatively simple model has profound implications for organizations and managerial leaders. What it suggests is that organizations are in a constant state of transition. It is not a short-term phenomenon, and it is not something you can manage on your way to creating the new status quo. Transition is the status quo, if that's possible. The ground is constantly moving under our feet, and it doesn't appear to be settling down any time soon.

F i g u r e   2.1

Managing change model—1970s.

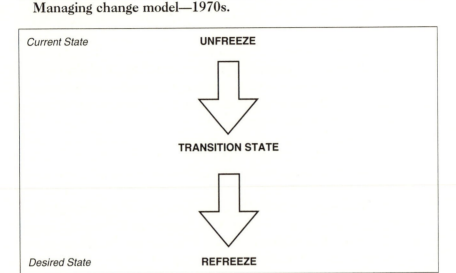

The constant motion and lack of stability causes serious discomfort for people working inside organizations. Human beings have a strong need for consistency and predictability in their environment—in other words, comfort. We like to be comfortable in our surroundings. I remember learning about homeostasis in eighth grade biology class. Defined as "the maintenance of a relatively stable state of equilibrium between interrelated physiological, psychological, or social factors characteristic of an individual or group," homeostasis is essential to attain, and the quest for homeostasis is a basic drive in all living organisms. It helps to explain why individuals stay in dysfunctional, abusive situations, whether at work or in their personal lives. People learn how to be "comfortable" even within a horrible set of circumstances. They know what is likely to happen, when it is likely to happen, and how it is likely to happen, and can thus prepare for it. However, there is no comfort in leaving a dysfunctional environment due to the fear of the unknown. A new environment might be worse—and would certainly be less predictable. As Pogo, the lovable comic strip character created by Walt Kelly, once said, "The certainty of misery is better than the misery of uncertainty." The desire for comfort is a very significant human motivator.

The lack of ability for people to find equilibrium among this barrage of constant change wreaks havoc in organizations. Discomfort leads to resistance and denial. "If it ain't broke, don't fix it" becomes a rallying cry. (The concept of "If it ain't broke, break it" is just as troublesome—change simply for the sake of change is intolerable amidst all the real reasons to change.) Resistance and denial lead to distrust of management and reduced levels of satisfaction. Dissatisfaction is demotivational, and it results in decreased productivity and decreased levels of performance. The leadership imperative is especially strong in this era of constant change and transition. There are leadership behaviors that make a difference in providing employees with an increased sense of comfort and stability—most notably those practices associated with emotional intelligence. As Alfred North Whitehead wrote, "The art of progress is to preserve order amid change, and change amid order."

Using the model shown in Figure 2.2, an analysis of the major forces of change that are driving business today will provide a richer understanding of how and why they impact your organization. The four principal forces include:

- Intense competition
- Demanding customers
- Technology
- Demanding shareholders

COMPETITION

It is difficult to identify an industry that is not experiencing intense competition. There is nothing new about having competitors in an industry, but the scope of competition and its ever-changing nature is continuously accelerating.

You don't need to look much further than at companies within industries that were historically heavily regulated—utilities, telecommunications, and banking, to name a few. The competitive

F i g u r e   2.2

Forces shaping change.

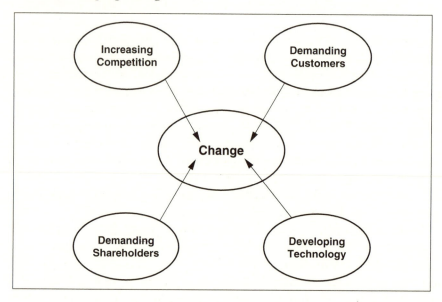

landscape is dramatically different today for those businesses. The leadership ramifications of the changing business environments are profound. Three cases in point:

SCANA Corporation

For many years, South Carolina Electric and Gas (SCE&G) operated as a traditional regulated electric utility company. It operated in a relatively small geographic area covering most of the state of South Carolina. When the natural gas industry deregulated in the eighties, SCANA Corporation (the holding company for SCE&G) got into the natural gas business and created a business unit that is currently known as SCANA Energy. This move opened up new markets for the company but also brought the company into a new world of competition. SCANA Energy learned how to compete in the nonregulated environment, and it developed its own corporate culture, quite distinct from that of SCE&G.

As the industry was moving toward deregulation in electricity, SCANA's competitors began changing—chiefly by expanding scale. Southern Company became the dominant utility in the Southeast, as it owned Georgia Power, Mississippi Power, and Alabama Power. Southern also became an international company, expanding into overseas activities. Duke Power, headquartered in Charlotte, North Carolina, also became a global utility and began to rapidly grow its business outside the United States. And in what was a truly telling "state of the industry" event, Duke Power merged with Enron of Texas—the mega natural gas company. What made this merger so extraordinary was the fact that for many years Duke Power had been aggressively marketing electricity as being far superior to natural gas as a source of power. The anti–natural gas culture at Duke Power was very apparent. By merging with Enron, Duke had become a natural gas provider.

Surrounded by Southern, Duke Energy, and Carolina Power & Light, SCANA was forced to look for new ways to compete if it were to remain an independent company. It was highly vulnerable to being acquired—SCANA's share price had been stagnant for an extended period of time, and yet the company had one of the lowest costs of production (based on megawatt-hours) in the industry. While its geographic area was small, it was attractively situated in the sunbelt and included the high tourist regions of Charleston and Myrtle Beach. Thus, mounting pressure at SCANA was not focused solely on winning business against its competitors. SCANA also felt intensely pressured because it had the potential of being acquired. SCANA experienced three CEO changes in less than five years, if more proof is needed of the intensity of its competitive environment.

Bank of America

I remember as a college student opening my first bank account in 1971 with NCNB, the Charlotte-based financial institution otherwise known as North Carolina National Bank. Having been raised in New York, I was familiar with the banking powerhouses of Chase Manhattan and Chemical Bank. Over the years, I have watched NCNB grow from a modest statewide institution to become NationsBank, a strong regional bank operating in multiple states through acquisitions, to its current global status as Bank of America. At the time of the merger between NationsBank and BankAmerica, it was larger than either Chase or Chemical (until they merged a few years ago in order to keep pace with the competition). All these changes transpired in less than 30 years under one CEO—Hugh McColl. But the intensity of competition that drove McColl when he was leading NCNB was not coming from the New York financial institutions. He had two principal rivals that were virtually next-door neighbors: First Union National Bank, which was also headquartered in Charlotte, and Wachovia, of nearby Winston-Salem, North Carolina. As interstate banking spread, the competitiveness among these three banks intensified. It was interesting to get to know their respective CEOs—three very different individuals whose personalities were clearly imprinted on their organizations.

John Medlin ran Wachovia in the keenly professional, conservative fashion consistent with his character. He was highly respected by his peers in the banking industry as a man of great principles and a sound financier. Wachovia was certainly the most conservative and slow-paced of the three North Carolina banks and also the most secure for many years.

Edwin Crutchfield, an exceptionally bright and private individual, led First Union. Crutchfield's competitiveness was highly focused on Hugh McColl's bank. Whenever NCNB built a new headquarters skyscraper in Charlotte, First Union would follow suit with a slightly taller building. Both banks entered the fast-growing Florida market. NCNB was rather heavy-handed in it's "in your face" approach. First Union was far more successful being more low-key, and it stayed away from the high-visibility areas of the gold coast of Florida, concentrating instead on Jacksonville. As bright as he was, Crutchfield was caught between the traditional banker, Medlin, and the highly aggressive former Marine, McColl. First Union's inability to keep pace with NationsBank became increasingly onerous, and the bank languished a bit as being more follower than leader.

My first meeting with Hugh McColl was during a recruiting visit at the University of North Carolina's business school. As an

MBA placement director, I had attended many corporate recruiting receptions where the executives put on a sales pitch for their firm to the students. Of course, few companies sent their CEO to participate in such an event, but UNC was NationsBank's largest source of managerial talent, and McColl was an alumnus. His presentation was unique and incredibly effective. McColl would simply stand on a chair that was placed in the middle of a large reception room and talk to the students about the bank and why they should want to be a part of it. As a relatively short man, standing on the chair enabled him to see everyone at one time. And the rather dramatic effect on the students of seeing a major CEO in this context was much more memorable than any slick PowerPoint presentation could ever be. McColl's talk was straight and to the point. He came across as a no-nonsense, tough-minded leader who valued his troops.

By the year 2000, Medlin and Crutchfield had retired, but McColl continued as chairman of Bank of America. Global banking is now the battlefield, with continuing consolidation across state and national boundaries. In April 2001, the (almost) unthinkable happened when First Union and Wachovia announced their intention to merge. Only time will tell how that potential marriage will affect the competitive landscape in financial services, but certainly in 1985 no one would have predicted how these three banks actually evolved by the beginning of the twenty-first century.

BellSouth

The telecommunications industry presents an even more remarkable story regarding intensification of competition over the past 10 years. The seemingly monumental challenges that were faced by the Baby Bells upon their creation from the AT&T divestiture seem somewhat trivial compared with the competitive issues BellSouth faces today. In the eighties and nineties, the greatest concern among these new telecommunications companies was how to transform their corporate mindset from the operational focus of the regulated world to a market focus in the competitive environment. The world of telecommunications changed slowly (at first) from incorporating just local and long-distance phone service to include cellular. Today, telecommunications firms are also involved in cable, Internet connectivity, satellite, broadband, and wireless personal communications devices.

BellSouth competes with an incredible array of communications-related companies—from AT&T, Sprint, and MCI Worldcom to Earthlink, AOL/Time Warner, and Deutsche Telekom. There is no way that telecommunications companies can compete as independent entities. They must form alliances and create joint ventures in order to generate the resources required to serve exploding markets with constant technological innovations. For example, I saw two advertisements on the same day that illustrated the incredible changes in telecommunications. One was promoting Cingular Wireless, the new joint-venture company recently created by SBC and BellSouth (two of the original Baby Bells) and nine other firms. Each of those companies had its own cellular business that it had been branding for years. Now, the companies have joined forces and are banking on establishing a new brand. In promoting Cingular's service, they offer a new Nokia phone for $10. Scandinavian-based Nokia has the widely recognized brand name, not Cingular (just ask Motorola). The other advertisement was for Deutsche Telekom—the German telecommunications giant. The company had placed an image ad in the southeast edition of the *New York Times*, promoting its capabilities across the telecommunications spectrum in providing local phone service, wireless, and high-speed Internet connections. Nokia and Deutsche Telekom were barely blips on BellSouth's radar screen 10 years ago. Cingular Wireless didn't exist until 2001.

Competition is global, and it is intensifying in every industry, for every organization. And most often, the competitors to be concerned about are the new ones—the firms you don't know much about. They are more likely to catch you by surprise than your traditional competitors.

CUSTOMERS

What a long way Ralph Nader has come from being one of the first, highly visible consumer advocates to becoming a third-party presidential candidate in the 2000 election. While one may not be able to point to him as the principal reason Al Gore lost that election, you can trace the rise in consumerism to Nader's efforts advocating for improved safety in the automobile industry three decades before. "Our customers are much more demanding than they have ever been" is a common lament of businesses today. In the context of B2C (business to consumer), customers should be demanding—especially in receiving value for their investment of time and money. Quality customer service is still lacking in this country despite all the attention it was paid in the eighties and nineties. There are few experiences I have as a consumer that come close to making my top 10 best customer service list. But it seems that every week I have an experience that could qualify for inclusion on my top 10 list of customer disservice horror stories.

The challenge of "demanding customers" is focused more on the B2B (business-to-business) side. Look at a hypothetical case: Company X faces tough times, with shrinking margins, rising costs of raw materials, and stiffer competition in the marketplace. The company is in a cost reduction mode, trying to squeeze every penny to the bottom line. Company Y is a major supplier to Company X. Guess whose margins are going to get squeezed as well? Give yourself 10 points if you guessed Company Y. Naturally, Company Y will wind up having to reduce its cost structure in order to salvage its margin for products delivered to Company X—so watch out Company Z!

This is not such a hypothetical example. Kemet Electronics produces component parts (condensers) used in manufacturing microchips. Intel is Kemet's most significant customer. The PC industry is suffering from overcapacity and intense price competition. Therefore, Intel has to keep its costs down as it produces processors for IBM, Dell, Compaq, and the other major PC manufacturers. The poor folks at Kemet don't stand a chance. They have to sell to Intel, and they have to meet their price points or Intel will buy from someone else. It's a commodity business that doesn't allow for premium pricing. The squeeze is on, and everyone at Kemet feels it.

This level of pressure from demanding customers goes well beyond the consumerism attributed to Nader. I don't know if the exceptionally demanding customer movement in the B2B arena can be traced to anyone in particular, but the merchandisers at Wal-Mart and Home Depot have perfected it to an art form. These companies blew apart Michael Porter's competitive advantage matrix (see Figure 2.3). There isn't much of a strategic choice left any more of being either the low-cost producer or the high-value-added differentiated provider. Just ask Wal-Mart or Home Depot suppliers — you have to be both low cost and high value added in order to survive!

TECHNOLOGY

This force is almost too obvious to talk about. If you look back in time, can you imagine the impact on business of the technological advances at the beginning of the twentieth century? From automobiles to telephones to mass production manufacturing, the effects on industrial organizations had to be extraordinary. Yet it appears to us that technology is having an unprecedented impact on business at the start of the twenty-first century. Perhaps all generations get caught in the trap that the dramas of their experiences are greater than those who came before. But it is hard to think of a time

Figure 2.3

Porter competitive strategy matrix.

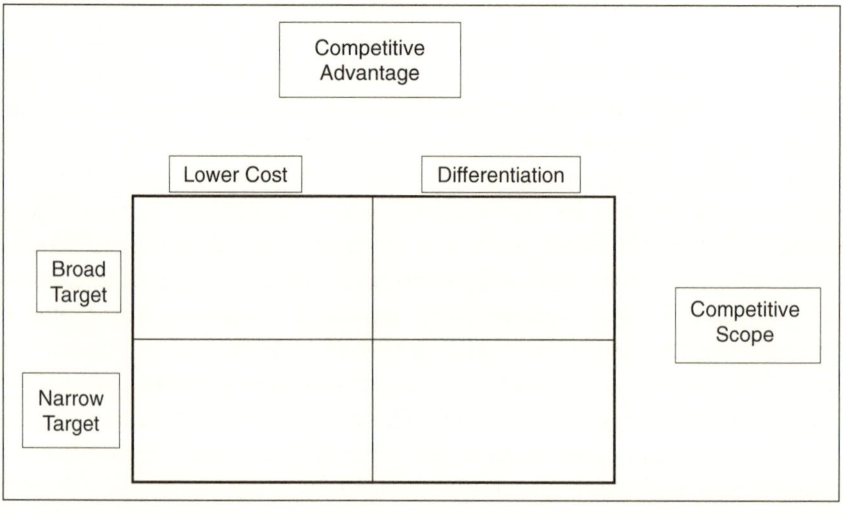

when technology had more influence on business than it does right now. It is pervasive, rapid-fire, and not just limited to one or two industries. The Internet alone lays an entirely new dimension on how business is conducted. All companies struggle to keep up with the advances. The difficulty lies in this rapid pace of technological change. Substantial investment is required in order to fully adopt a new technology, in terms of both finances and human resources. By the time the investment is ready to generate a return, the adopted technology has become obsolete, turning a competitive advantage into a significant strategic constraint before it ever had an opportunity to be sufficiently leveraged as an advantage.

However, the impact of technology on our products and services is only a part of the picture. There is an equally significant impact on the way we do business—how people in organizations work together in order to produce and deliver products and services. Geography is becoming increasingly irrelevant, as we are able to conduct business, real time, from very distant locations. But group dynamics and human behaviors are still extremely relevant to the productive use of technology.

Case in point: I was involved in a consulting project with Glaxo, the British pharmaceutical firm, prior to the mergers with Burroughs Wellcome and SmithKline. The American-based research and development group was expanding rapidly and had begun to challenge its British colleagues for influence and power within the company. In the political battles that were waged, it became clear to the executives in charge of R&D that they could not afford to operate the labs as independent entities. When they included the research scientists working on developing new medicines in other parts of the world, the need for a global solution became even more apparent. With the enhancements in communications technologies, Glaxo was able to create virtual R&D teams that were composed of scientists spread across continents. Real collaboration could occur on scientific discoveries that were heretofore unthinkable without having people physically located in the same laboratory. However, technology is not the end result but simply a means to the ends. What the U.S. scientists discovered was that the collaborative process had to be engineered as carefully as the technology itself. Having the ability to work together on discovering new medicines while living in different regions of the world is not sufficient in and of itself. The Americans had learned that the human dynamics were the most important to focus on first—building the collaborative teamwork and decision making processes was critical to successful utilization of the enabling technology.

DEMANDING SHAREHOLDERS

For all the strength behind technology as a force of change, it doesn't equal the power that the dramatic rise in shareholder influence has had on U.S. corporations over the past 20 years. With the great increase in institutional investing, companies have been forced to provide higher returns to shareholders than ever before. Don't get me wrong. I am not opposed to the concept of providing the highest possible return to shareholders. But that concept has developed claws and fangs, and it is ripping at the flesh of many corporations. The imperative to meet expectations in delivering short-term earnings has forced executives to sacrifice sustainability for quick (oftentimes fleeting) returns. Analysts exert extraordinary influence as they issue their buy-sell-hold recommendations. They are primarily interested in two metrics from companies, regardless of their industry or markets: predictability and growth. Predictability is important to give confidence to investors—in the sense that the company meets its earnings projections each quarter. Growth is important to provide better returns to shareholders. Many investment options are available today. To attract investment dollars, companies have to produce higher returns than the returns from any of the safer, more stable investment vehicles in order to combat the increased risk. Thus, growth becomes the other imperative. Dividends were appealing in the past as a vehicle for providing some incremental income for investors and as indicators of successful earnings. Most investors now view dividends as constraining growth, as the dividends tie up potential investment capital in new business opportunities in order to distribute some of the company's earnings among its shareholders.

Growth and predictability do not go hand in hand. Sometimes, it is quite the contrary. Companies that continually hit rather conservative earnings projections achieve consistency, but they do not grow—thus, their stock price languishes unenthusiastically. Corporations that pursue aggressive growth strategies will often wind up with inconsistent swings in earnings as they take risks and climb the learning curve. This erodes predictability—thus, risk-averse investors adversely affect their stock prices. As stock prices suffer, so does investor confidence, and eventually the capital available to sustain growth begins to dry up. It is a difficult cycle to break. Just ask any director of investor relations at firms whose P/E ratios haven't improved much over the past five years.

We could add more to the forces-of-change model—powerful influencers such as government regulation, environmentalism, and work force dynamics—but for the sake of looking at the leadership implications of change, these four (competition, customers, technology, and shareholders) adequately paint the picture of tumultuous, relentless change acting on any and all midsized to large corporations.

QUESTIONS AND EXERCISES

- Draw a map of your industry that identifies key competitors with regard to their relative size and market power. Where does your company fall on the map? What are the implications of this position? What are the barriers to entry in your industry? Who are the potentially significant new competitors?

- Create a 2 × 2 matrix, with your key customers listed vertically and your firm's product-service portfolio running horizontally. Rate each customer's attachment to your company on a scale of 1–5 for each part of the portfolio that the individual customers utilize. How diversified are your ties with your key customers? How hard do you have to work to serve their needs and maintain their loyalty? Where will your new customers come from?

- Reflect on the past five years—over that period of time, how has technology changed the way your organization functions and serves its customers? How has the Internet affected your business to date? What technological advances can you foresee coming that will significantly impact your industry?

- Briefly profile your company's primary shareholders. What are their investment objectives? How much influence do they currently exert? If your organization is not publicly traded, identify the key stakeholders. How influential are they in the day-to-day operations? How might the influence of the key shareholders or stakeholders change in the next five years?

- With this level of analysis of the forces acting upon your company, what must the organization do differently in order to effectively address these influences? Where do you fit into that picture?

CHAPTER 3

Organizations That Thrive in Chaos

> *"The question that faces the strategic decision-maker is not 'what his organization should do tomorrow.' It is, 'what do we have to do today to be ready for an uncertain tomorrow'?"*
>
> — Peter Drucker

Most companies are struggling to cope with the barrage of constant change. Just when the situation seems to be settling down a bit, the next wave hits and the organization must react and make a new series of adjustments. While it seems to the associates that their company is uniquely facing these challenges, the reality is that virtually all organizations are caught up in this constantly reactive state.

In the many course sessions that I have conducted on "change management" in the past few years, I have frequently asked the participants to describe an organization that not only would survive in the tumultuous state of transition that all companies face, but would thrive in this dynamic environment. The consistency in the descriptions across these many groups of such an organization is impressive. The prototype that they discern is clear—the company that thrives amidst this chaos is:

- *Flexible.* The organization would be adept at shifting resources to meet changing environmental influences. Regardless of size, it would operate as a small company, without bureaucracy.
- *Fast.* Speed wins in business today. The organization would be able to move fast to respond to new market demands. Multiple layers of management would not impede its abili-

ty to make quick decisions and slow it down. Information and resources would flow expeditiously to the appropriate locations to enable fast response to problems and opportunities.

- *Empowered.* Decision making authority would be at the field level where the employees closest to the action would be able to respond to local changes without having to wait for approval from the home office.

- *Open in its communications.* There would be open communication channels that promoted the timely distribution of information across levels of the organization. Bad news would be able to travel up the organizational chart without fear of retribution. Communication filtering would be minimal, and the company would be effective at getting the right information to the right people at the right time.

- *Innovative.* The organization would operate in an environment that supported risk taking and rewarded innovation. As opposed to incremental continuous improvement, the company would experience leaps in new product development and process advances.

- *Learning-oriented.* The organizational culture would support and promote institutional learning. Knowledge coming in to the company would be systematically captured, stored, and disseminated throughout the enterprise to best leverage the new information to enhance performance.

- *Development-focused.* There would be a pervasive leadership style that focused on human resource development. The organization would realize that if it were to accomplish its objectives, it would need people who never stopped learning and enhancing their skills. The company would support a comprehensive portfolio of learning activities and job rotations to help each associate fully develop his or her talents.

- *Lean.* No room for layers of fat in this organization. Nor would the company be emaciated, either, as it would have sufficient resources to accomplish its objectives. Costs would be contained, and all financial and human resources would be fully optimized to provide the best possible return to shareholders.

- *Energized.* This would be a high-energy environment with high levels of activity and enthusiasm. Associates would be committed to the organization and to each other in accomplishing their goals. It would be a fun and exciting place to work.

- *Team-oriented.* No room for self-serving associates in this organization. Everyone would be focused on the organization's performance—all would be working effectively together to achieve their common purpose and holding each other accountable.

- *Performance-based.* The company's activities would be built around performance. Success in the marketplace would be the associates' best assurance of job security. All employees would be accountable to produce to their fullest potential. Winning would be concentrated fully on external competitors rather than on internal battles fighting for resources and recognition.

- *Values-driven.* Along with a focus on performance, the organization would incorporate a strong set of values to provide stability and consistency for all associates while they operate in a highly dynamic business environment. Hitting the numbers would not be sufficient for reward and promotion. Managers and executives would have to "live the values," as well as achieve results, in order to be recognized for their overall contributions.

Wouldn't anyone be thrilled to work for this company? Certainly, all the participants I have had in my courses would want to. You can see it on their faces as they describe this ideal organization—a combination of zest, longing, and remorse that it is just an ideal rather than a reality.

My response to them is to make this more reality than ideal by using it as their organizational vision for the part of the company that is within their sphere of influence. Yes, it is difficult to operate in this progressive fashion when your unit is inside a more repressive larger organization. But it is not impossible. Even if you cannot get all the way there, moving in the direction of the type of company that thrives in chaos could only be positive. You have to find ways to build a culture in your corner of the organization that is more flexible, empowered, development-focused, innovative, and learning-oriented. And it is certainly appropriate to operate under a strong set of values with which everyone can identify as the unit focuses on performance.

Case in point: I tried to follow this organizational model during my five years as director of the Daniel Management Center (DMC) at the University of South Carolina's Darla Moore School of Business. The unit had been operating primarily as a broker of outside consultants. New leadership wanted to see the school elevate all its activities, and so I was hired to make the DMC more of an executive education organization inside a major business school. Resistance was high throughout the institution. The DMC staff were not interested in change. The rest of the school was struggling with complacency, and the university as a whole was stuck in the past. Fortunately, a few key faculty members were highly supportive of the changes we wanted to make in the DMC. They invested a good bit of time in helping me transform the Center. More faculty came on board as we gained momentum in attracting new corporate clients and ratcheting up the program portfolio.

To add to the Center's flexibility, I hired a few new staff members who brought new skills and perspectives into the organization. We worked hard at reducing the cycle time for introducing new programs in order to become faster in responding to customer needs. I reorganized the Center into business units to provide associates with more complete roles in servicing clients coupled with heightened accountability. We experimented with new educational media, including satellite delivery of executive education sessions, in order to keep pace with the dynamic changes in our industry.

The Center had been well known for repeating the same mistakes over and over again. It was a reactive organization with no teamwork and a lost sense of pride. It took longer than I had hoped, but by the end of my term this had turned around quite a bit. Regular debriefings were held after programs to address problems that arose. Numerous "process reengineering" sessions were scheduled to work on improving workflow and customer service.

I was fortunate to hire a former graduate assistant from the Master of Human Resources program to serve in a senior management position at the Center. Her skills in building work teams and keeping everyone concentrating on performance were critically important to the Center's evolution. Through all this, we kept a consistent focus on customer service and return on investment as the value drivers of the business.

Was it a total success? No, but great progress was made over the five years. The Center became the leading edge of the school's progress and helped create new corporate partnerships that were indicative of this heightened level. But as with many other organizations in similar situations, the foundation for this transformed DMC was fragile, and after I left, it all started to come apart when the school experienced another change in its leadership at the top. The lesson learned for me was that change may be simple, but it's never easy. When it comes to being a change agent, you have to realize that momentum is hard to get, hard to keep, and easy to lose. But this experience, among others, helped me understand that you can lead change at the middle-management level inside a complex organization. Focusing on the organizational characteristics cited earlier in the chapter would be a great way to start. But before you begin making things happen, you need to thoroughly understand the human side of change—particularly, why people resist change and how you can work to overcome that resistance. The next chapter takes a pragmatic look at these issues.

QUESTIONS AND EXERCISES

- What are your organization's espoused values? How are they brought to life every day? What are the values that drive you in your job? How are they aligned with your organization's values?
- Draw a continuum with the end points being "static and inflexible" on the left and "highly dynamic and flexible" on the right. Where does your company fall on this continuum? How close to the midpoint?
- Now plot the point on the continuum that best describes your unit. Is there any difference between your unit's position and your company's position? Where should your unit's position be on the continuum?
- Describe all the formal programs and informal processes your company uses to promote learning. Next, identify all the formal and informal organizational impediments to learning. Which list is longer? What are the implications of this imbalance?
- How can you change the environment so as to encourage more learning occurring across the organization?

CHAPTER 4

$$\text{Overcoming Resistance}$$

"But, oh! the heavy change, now thou art gone,
Now thou art gone, and never must return!"
— John Milton

When is the last time you experienced a major change in your personal life? Think about what you went through emotionally during that period. Over the past 18 months, at the tender age of 47, I moved from Columbia, South Carolina, to Atlanta as a single parent with three school-age children; started a new, very challenging job; experienced the death of one of my parents; sent my daughter off to college for the first time; and met the love of my life, got married, and merged families that involved blending a total of four teenage boys and four cats into one household. It was a set of experiences that easily measured 9.8 on the Richter scale. And, yes, there are continuing aftershocks! I believe I am pretty adaptive and open to change. But this level of change is intense, and I find myself having to work very hard to make the appropriate adjustments. Getting older doesn't help, either. Certainly, I have more maturity than I had 15 years ago, but my aversion to risk is growing while my energy level is declining. Fortunately, almost all the changes I experienced were for the better. Therefore, it was helpful to keep myself focused on a positive vision of where I was heading. Still, it was very challenging emotionally.

It occurs to me that my personal experience is analogous to what happens to many people in their work environments. Different issues, obviously, but the quantity and depth of change are similar to what a number of organizations have experienced over the past few years.

Case in point: Recently, a technician from Comcast, the cable company that serves our neighborhood, came to my house. I had enrolled in its new service that provided cable access for high-speed Internet connectivity and the system went down. The tech support over the phone didn't solve the problem, so I requested a service call. Lewis, the technician, was wearing an AT&T emblem on his shirt when I opened the door. It startled me a bit, as I couldn't imagine why an AT&T repairman was at the house. When I asked why he was wearing that shirt, Lewis replied that AT&T had acquired Comcast just a few days ago. He was not particularly pleased with that outcome, as he had purposely chosen to work for a small, somewhat entrepreneurial company. Now, beyond his control, Lewis was part of the huge AT&T global corporation. He also was working in a technical area that was new to him. The cable company had just started offering the Internet connectivity service, and Lewis had to be retrained in order to provide technical support to his customers. He did not seem to be overly stressed about the changes, "but it's a lot to deal with," as Lewis so aptly stated. The aura of resignation to the powers of fate, more than a sense of tension, was most striking to me about Lewis's reactions to his work situation. It made me wonder what I could do to help him if I were his manager. What would you do?

To answer that question it is important to understand both why people resist change and what is the likely range of behavioral consequences of that resistance. Here is my list of reasons why resistance to change is so prevalent in the workplace:

- *Fear of the unknown.* The basic human need to achieve comfort in one's environment has already been discussed. Change implies uncertainty, and uncertainty is uncomfortable. Not knowing what may potentially happen often leads to heightened anxiety. Most people will do whatever they can to reduce their levels of anxiety. Resisting change is one of these anxiety-reducing actions.
- *Fear of failure.* The new order may require skills and abilities that are beyond our capabilities. Since we know how to operate in the existing order, there is resistance to trying a new approach. We may fail. When word processing first came into the workplace, most secretaries were adamantly resistant. They saw no reason to learn how to use a computer when they were very efficient in using the typewriter. Would anyone go back to typewriters now? But the fear of

not being able to learn the new technology generated a lot of resistance to giving up traditional typing at the time.

- *Not understanding the need for change.* This concern is related to the expression "If it ain't broke, don't fix it" that was previously mentioned. A common perspective among associates in companies that are facing sudden, significant change is the lack of a felt need for the change. "We've been successful going the way we've been going, so why do we suddenly need to follow a very different path?" is the frequently asked question.

- *Disagreement with the need for change.* A closely related factor that causes resistance to change is the feeling among associates that the new direction is the wrong direction. It's not that they don't understand the reasoning behind the changes, but rather that they believe the reasoning is flawed. This is particularly commonplace in organizations that have generated high levels of skepticism from a track record of frequent and ineffective change initiatives. *Total quality, continuous process improvement, self-directed work teams,* and *learning organizations* are all buzzwords that became synonymous with "program of the month" at many companies across the country. The decisions made to pursue any of these movements often lacked total commitment, were poorly thought out and wound up being ineffectively implemented. I recall talking with one manufacturing associate who was describing his displeasure at the new total quality management program that his company was initiating—"this, too, shall pass" was his parting comment. It was clear to me that he was never going to invest any energy or effort in the TQM program. And lacking clear reasoning for why he should, or how the company was going to be fully committed to the effort, why should he buy into the change process?

- *Losing something of value.* Ultimately it will come down to the infamous acronym WIIFM (what's in it for me?). You can talk all you want to about the strategic imperatives and the complexities of doing business in the global environment, but all that associates really want to know is how the change will affect them. If you do not communicate to them at that level, you will never get them to buy in. If people believe they will wind up losing as a result of the change, they will resist. The more significant the perceived loss, the more vigorous the resistance. Imagine a VP who has been with the company for 20 years and just recently made it to the executive level where he runs a major division. In the new restructuring plan, this division is dissolved and winds up being spread among various other business units. What type of resistance would you anticipate from the VP? Given his positional power, imagine how influential that resistance could be to undermining the change initiative.

- *Inertia.* Don't underestimate the power of fatigue and burnout. Change requires effort. Oftentimes, it requires significant effort. And aging takes its toll on our desire and energy reserves. Sometimes you can fully understand the need for change, believe that it is the right thing to do for the company, see your potential gain, and know that you could do it well—if only you had it in you to try it one more time. All things being equal, people will choose the path of least resistance if they are provided with the option. And that path would lead to not putting forth the effort to change. We all have our limits for how much change we can bear, and many people are close to, or over, their limit.

Let's go back to the cable technician, Lewis. Which factors might influence his resistance to change? It didn't appear to me that he has a fear of failure even though he is supporting a new technology. Nor can I imagine the issues of not understanding the need for change, or disagreeing with the need for change, to be operating on him. However, Lewis showed me signs of fearing the unknown as he talked about his concerns about working for a large corporation. Similarly, he probably is worried about losing something of value in this switch—with the loss being less control of his destiny and having less of a presence in an organization the size of AT&T.

The question posed was how could we help Lewis feel more comfortable with this change and be a more satisfied, motivated employee? The answer lies in the strategies that can be employed to overcome the various forms of resistance to change. Once there is an understanding of where an individual's resistance comes from, it is possible to work through the resistance. Here are some techniques you can apply for each of the major factors described above.

FEAR OF THE UNKNOWN

The best approach to overcome fear of the unknown is to help the person envision a positive future. You may not be able to paint a complete picture of where the organization is headed, but you should at least be able to articulate a vision of the direction in which the company is going. The main point is to communicate that the new direction is the right direction—and that if the company just stayed on the old path, it would eventually lead to serious decline. For Lewis, I would talk with him about the realities of a small company remaining small amidst all the consolidation in the telecommunications industry. It would be highly unlikely that Comcast could remain independent, and therefore it was good that a solid firm, such as AT&T, was the acquirer. Clearly, the company wants to be a major player in the cable and broadband sectors of the telecom industry and has the resources to do so.

FEAR OF FAILURE

In addressing concerns over the fear of failure, it is important to help individuals develop confidence that they will fit into the new order. In this context, it is particularly important to be encouraging and positive rather than authoritarian (the "my way or the highway" approach). No one should expect to be highly effective right away when working in a new situation. Everyone needs to climb the learning curve—some just do it faster than others, but most people are capable of getting there eventually. Statements that indicate patience with their initial limited success, show support for their continuing learning, and express confidence in their ability to perform are all important in helping people overcome their anxieties at work. Training and development initiatives are excellent tactics to utilize to demonstrate the company's willingness to invest in their associates' learning what they need to learn to be effective in the new environment.

NOT UNDERSTANDING THE NEED FOR CHANGE

Communication is the key to overcoming the resistance generated by a lack of understanding the need for change. Here it is important to assess the individual's preferred communications style, if you are working with just one person. Does the individual respond better to a rational-logical argument that analyzes the pros and cons of change? Or is this someone who reacts better to passionate discourse with an emphasis on the emotional side of the need for change? If you are going to be meeting with a group, you would want to make a similar assessment and try to determine which style was more at play with the members. If the balance is close to 50-50, you should design your presentation to cover both perspectives—the rational and the emotional components. Not understanding the need for change is the predominant reason for resistance to change in larger organizations. What appears obvious in the executive suite regarding the compelling reasons to change does not make its way down to the ground level very effectively. And when the top-down communications strategy is built around emails that announce changes rather than face-to-face dialogs that focus on the reasons for changing, there is a serious disconnect across organizational levels.

This lack of understanding that results from poor communication down the organization is so common that it is the most serious barrier to effective change management in corporations today. You have to make sure you are communicating the need for change in a way the person can understand it, which could be very different from the way you understand it. This is why supervisors or frontline managers play such a critical role in organizational transformation. They are the lynchpin between management and employees. Supervisors speak the language that employees can understand; after all, most of them were formerly hourly associates who were promoted to supervisory roles. Managers typically don't speak this language and therefore are not effective in their communications about change. If you want the nonexempt employees to understand the reasons behind a major change initiative, you must focus attention on the frontline supervisors. They will be the key to getting the message down the chain.

Case in point: The Medical University of South Carolina (MUSC) was experiencing a time of enormous change in the mid-nineties. The whole health-care industry was in the midst of a revolution, but public hospitals were even more under duress. Columbia HCA was gobbling up hospitals across the country, and it had set its sights on the hospital that was affiliated with MUSC . Negotiations were under way to "sell" the hospital (not the medical school) to Columbia HCA. Just a few months prior to the beginning of these negotiations, MUSC had experienced its first-ever reduction in force due to significant budgetary distress. Employee morale was sinking fast. The hospital was based in Charleston, and most of the employee population came from impoverished, minority communities in surrounding townships that have traditionally served the wealthy Charlestonian society. Employees felt a strong sense of distrust of those in power, as well as an intense feeling of entitlement as public employees of the state of South Carolina that their jobs should be completely secure. While the negotiations with HCA were going on, rumors were flying throughout the hospital that many jobs would be eliminated and that everyone would suffer from pay cuts or loss of benefits. As you might imagine, patient care was suffering as a result of the high levels of organizational distress.

Adding to its woes, MUSC was trying to create multidisciplinary teams to help provide higher-quality service while more effectively leveraging its resources. Its competitors were moving fast in creating community-based delivery systems that were more responsive to the unique needs of the local citizens. It was clear to the hospital's administrators that they had to change the way they thought about delivering medical care, treating patients, and managing their human and capital assets. Initial efforts to build cooperation across clinics and to improve customer satisfaction ratings from patients were completely ineffective. Hal, one of the senior administrators, came to the realization that the ongoing negotiations with HCA were paralyzing the organization. The employees' inability to understand what was going on, why all these changes were being made, and what the impact would be on them created a highly dysfunctional atmosphere that prevented any and all progress on their other initiatives. Hal came up with a communications strategy that focused on the midlevel managers and supervisors—a group that predominantly consisted of the nurses who ran the clinics and managed the work force. He figured that by making sure these managers were fully informed about what was happening, they would be the key to communicating the information accurately to the employees. Hal convinced the other senior administrators to hold weekly "communications meetings." Every Tuesday afternoon, from 2 to 3 o'clock, members of the senior team met with all 50+ midlevel managers and supervisors in the auditorium. The members of the senior team provided updates at the beginning of each meeting, sharing the latest information they could regarding the potential merger. Many times, there was information that could not be provided, as it would have been in violation of the rules for the negotiations. At these times, the senior group would tell the managers what little news they could share and explain why they could not say more. Then, they would open the floor for questions, and they urged the managers to raise questions they were hearing from the employees.

It was not easy to schedule everyone at a set time each week, but the meetings became so important that everyone made a commitment to be there. Many of the managers and senior administrators point to the beginning of those weekly communications meetings as the key turning point in the struggling change process. Eventually the negotiations with HCA were terminated, as the state legislature decided not to approve the merger. However, the effort put into the communications meetings had a long-lasting positive impact on the organization.

DISAGREEMENT WITH THE NEED FOR CHANGE

When people's resistance to change is driven by their disagreeing with the need for change, or with the direction the change represents, it is important to make sure they feel their concerns are heard. Listening is the principal tactic to employ. Most people just want to be listened to—to believe their opinion matters and that someone in authority cares enough to hear them out. There is no harm in giving them that opportunity. First of all, you might learn something you didn't know. Perhaps, they have information you don't have. And they may provide you with clues about how others might be thinking. Finally, listening helps to build trust, and you will need to gain their trust as the change process unfolds. The downside to letting people ventilate is that it is time-consuming and potentially irritating. For those who continue to insist that the company is wrong in moving in the new direction, you eventually have to help them come to a decision. You can acknowledge that their view is understandable but then firmly point out that the company has made its decision and it is time to either get on board with it or leave the organization. The individuals who disagree don't have to be convinced that they are wrong, only that they need to support the decision that has been made.

LOSING SOMETHING OF VALUE

To address people's resistance to change due to the perception that they are losing something of value, you must first be honest. They may be right, and to attempt to persuade them that they are not losing anything does nothing but destroy your credibility. They will stop listening and continue resisting. It is important to try to determine what is being lost—money, power, job security? Then, acknowledge their notion of loss, but try to help the individuals see the issue from a different perspective. Perhaps the loss would be greater if they continued resisting. And help them think about what they have to gain from becoming a positive part of the change process rather than a detriment. During the period when many manufacturing companies were changing from traditional shifts to team-based processes, supervisors saw themselves as the ones with the most to lose. The traditional role of the supervisor is to tell the hourly associates what to do—a command-and-control style was predominant. After all, the supervisors had been hourly associates themselves and had been told what do to by their supervisors. Now when it was finally their turn to be in command, the company decided to switch to team-based activities. Instead of the supervisor telling the associates what to do, the team members were charged with deciding the assignments. Team members did the hiring, discipline, and firing in many circumstances. The supervisory role shifted from authoritarian to team facilitator. As a result most supervisors felt that the use of work teams was simply a way to get rid of them without doing so directly. Once the teams learned how to manage themselves, supervisors were redundant (or so the supervisors thought).

I found this attitude prevalent among a group of supervisors in a plant I was assisting to develop a team-based approach to their processes. It was clear that most of the supervisors were scared about losing their jobs and convinced that the whole initiative was specifically designed to make them quit rather than be fired. Over the course of several conversations, I learned that in addition to their fear of losing something of value (their jobs!), most of the supervisors were also afraid of failing as team facilitators. They knew how to be supervisors, in the traditional sense, but they didn't have a clue of how to be effective team leaders.

I counseled the plant manager to meet with the supervisors one-on-one to discuss the reasons behind the change process and to explain how important their contribution was to its overall success. The supervisors were informed that they would in no way lose their jobs if they were positive contributors and proponents of the team approach. Then the HR manager followed up and explained that the supervisors would be receiving comprehensive training in how to facilitate work teams to help them develop the necessary skills to be successful. It was also pointed out to each supervisor that the world of work had changed in most manufacturing facilities across the country. A lot of companies were developing team-based organizations, and so it would be very beneficial to each of the supervisors to learn how to be effective team leaders. Even if they left the company, it would make them much more marketable if they ever wanted to find another job in manufacturing. Most of the supervisors understood the situation and committed themselves to becoming good team leaders. The few who did not see the light were ineffective and were eventually let go by the company. While they undoubtedly blamed their terminations on the change process, it was their own resistance and inflexibility that caused them to lose their jobs.

Go back to Lewis, the cable technician, who also thought he would be losing something of value with AT&T's acquisition of Comcast. He's right to be concerned that size could add layers of bureaucracy to his organization, but what might he be gaining? AT&T will be able to offer him more extensive technical training. Since it is a much larger company, there are many more opportunities for career growth and options to transfer to new positions or new locations. And AT&T has a greater brand name than Comcast Communications, so it will carry more weight on his résumé should Lewis ever look for a new job with another company. In this instance, he stands to gain a lot more than he stands to lose.

INERTIA

There is no one best way to overcome the influence of inertia as a force of resistance to change. However, it is clear that the amount of energy and enthusiasm that you bring to the office will have a tremendous influence on your associates' attitudes. Hard-core cynicism is built up from years of bad experiences, and it is very difficult to overcome it in one leap. The best you might hope for is to help someone become less cynical and thus less cancerous in the organization for everyone else's benefit. But if you do not demonstrate energetic support for the change effort, do not expect your subordinates to do so. They learn from you and are heavily influenced by your actions—however unfair that might sound.

I vividly remember one manager who was an actuary in a major insurance company. David had been working at the firm for over 25 years and was clearly in the twilight of his career. He had a wealth of knowledge about the company and the industry, but he had become very cynical over the past five years—so much so that a job was created for David that kept him isolated from most others in the firm. Of course, this made him even more cynical. Why he continued to work with the company, or why the company hadn't asked him to retire, is still beyond me. It was an organization that had a strong nonconfrontational culture. All the battles fought inside were done covertly, never openly. And David struck me as someone who was very driven by comfort—he had become comfortable playing the cynic role, and he was undoubtedly afraid to try something new. Then, the company decided it needed to dramatically change its culture—to be more open, supportive, and empowering. David did not buy into it at all. While he agreed with those values, he did not believe that the company's leadership was seriously committed to changing the status quo. David was assigned to attend one of the first one-week leadership development programs I designed to support this change initiative. He started the program with a poor attitude, but when he saw the sincere commitment to change among a number of the members of the senior leadership team, David's perspective began to change. By the last session of the week, David showed tremendous progress. Several of his peers noticed the change in his behavior and told him how much they wanted him to become a contributing member of the organization again. It was a very meaningful week to David and one that propelled him to finish his time at the company in a much more productive and gratifying way.

One part of being an effective change agent is to take more of a proactive stance to minimize the impact that resistance carries. David would have not become quite so cynical if he had felt more a part of the organization's new direction than an outcast whose opinions were unimportant. There are ways to promote acceptance to change, especially for those who have Theory Y leanings. Here are a few proactive tactics that should assist you in gaining buy-in:

1. Bring people in early. The longer you wait to discuss the need for change with associates, the more they will distrust what you are doing to them. View this as an ongoing series of dialogs rather than a finished product you are delivering to the staff. Change is a continuous process, and everyone should feel a part of what is happening.

2. If you are coming into your organization as a new manager, take a little time to assess the current situation and then set up an aggressive timetable for making major changes. The longer you wait to break the status quo, the more resistant people will become to change. On the other hand, making sudden dramatic changes without having spent

any time understanding the organizational dynamics is unwise. This limits your credibility with the associates, as they will believe that you have your own agenda and that you are inclined to act first and ask questions later.

3. Identify the individuals who are most receptive to change. Start with the people who are most likely to respond positively to operating differently and help them to demonstrate success. If you spend all your energy on the heavy resistors, you won't have any left for the associates who are ready to change. This will turn off your best potential internal advocates.

4. Avoid bashing the way things have been done in the past. This is an easy trap to fall into, especially if you are taking over a unit that has been struggling. If you are too critical of the ways in which the unit has been functioning, you are denigrating the staff. As you get started, find a way to acknowledge that the way things were done in the past was probably appropriate for the situation at that time. Then help the associates to see that the future will require new practices and keep their attention focused forward, not backward.

5. In similar fashion, be careful not to talk a lot about the way you did things in your previous position. It is very irritating to listen to someone constantly saying things like "Well, when I was in sales, we did things this way. " The typical reaction people have to this type of comment is "Why don't you go back to sales if it was such a better place?" A different way to make your point, without aggravating your associates, is to say "From my experiences, I have learned that. . . ."

6. Get everyone involved in creating the new organization. There are two ingredients to keep in mind when pushing for change: the quality of the decision made about how to do things differently and the commitment people will have to execute that decision. The chances are high that you will be more concerned with implementation than with finding the one best answer. For example, make sure the people

who have to execute a new process are the ones helping to design it. Their ownership over the change will increase exponentially the more they believe they have control over the change. If you are concerned that your associates are incapable of coming up with an improved process, help them to learn how to do it. I have facilitated process reengineering sessions in organizations both to fix a specific process and to teach them a framework for addressing process improvement in the future.

A very important element in the change process is to build trust among the associates rather than destroy it. The more the associates feel respected and integrated into the new order, the more they will embrace change. These simple steps can help you build trust if you act with sincerity.

QUESTIONS AND EXERCISES

- Consider a time when you were resistant to a change at work. What were the circumstances? Why were you resisting? What was the outcome?
- If your organization is currently undergoing change, see the change matrix illustrated in Figure 4.1. Where does your company fall in the matrix—is resistance to change high or low? How fast must change occur for the organization to succeed?
- Identify the change management strategy most appropriate for where your organization falls in this matrix. How could you use this to help promote effective change in your part of the organization?

F i g u r e   4.1

Organizational change matrix.

	high	educational (skills)	rational logical
Receptivity to Change			
	low	force	educational (felt need)
		high	low

Time Pressure for Change

CHAPTER 5

Being in the Middle

"Somebody has to do something. . .
and it is just incredibly pathetic
that it has to be us."
— Jerry Garcia

One of the most critical challenges for a managerial leader is to learn how to be a change agent in the midst of an organization that does not truly want to change. You didn't create the mess that the company is in, nor are you the one determining where to go from here. However, you are held accountable for following the new plans, whether or not you agree with them. And the pièce de résistance—what I have just preached to you—is that your attitude is critical to the success of the new order. So you can't even let anyone see that you think it's all a bunch of baloney! Welcome to life in the middle.

Just like a middle child in a family of three kids, you wind up developing skills that neither the one above you nor the one below you has to develop. My son Jason knows this intimately as the middle child between his older sister and younger brother. He is a diplomat and seeks peaceful negotiations with warring parties. Jason believes he gets blamed for everything even though nothing is his fault (according to his reports). Thus, he has learned to be somewhat manipulative of the truth—but in his mind it's all for a good cause, as Jason sees himself as chiefly responsible for the welfare of the family. As such, he wants to know everything that is going on.

Sounds like the classic experience of the middle manager in an organization encountering significant change. Just like Jason, the middle manager has essential chores, such as cleaning the litter box and taking out the garbage. How do most people respond to this set of circumstances? For many it is very tempting to point upward and wait for "them" (senior executives) to get their act together before investing the energy in the hard work required to support organizational transformation. But if middle managers wait for the golden tablets to come down from the mountaintop, they will be waiting for a long time and no progress will be made. Of course, the supervisors below are similarly looking upward, pointing to the middle managers and blaming "them" as the obstacles to moving forward. It can always be viewed as someone else's responsibility. Ultimately, all of us are responsible for making it work, so don't wait for "them" to tell you what to do. Just do what you know is right, and the example you set will help others to act as well. The description in Chapter 3 of the ideal organization that would thrive in a state of constant transition provides a road map for doing what is right as a manager in the middle. Focus your efforts on transforming your area along each of the dimensions and you will make significant progress.

LEADING FOR CHANGE

Start with *flexibility*. Several years ago I was talking with a senior vice president at Wal-Mart about that company's ability to sustain success in the highly competitive retail industry. One comment in particular stood out among the many reasons he cited. "We try to build in flexibility with every decision that we make," he reported. That's quite a challenge given that among the major decisions are where to locate new Wal-Mart superstores. It's hard to be flexible when you invest in such a capital-intensive fixed asset. Yet that is exactly what the Wal-Mart executives strive for, and the fact that they have flexibility as one of their primary concerns by itself makes Wal-Mart more flexible than most of its competitors.

How can you adopt a similar philosophy—can you look for ways to build in flexibility as you make business decisions? It is certainly possible to do so regarding staffing decisions. I have learned that it is usually wiser to hire people who are good generalists than those who are outstanding specialists. Our industry is also experiencing major changes, and it is hard to predict with any precision what types of competencies my staff members will need to have for us to be successful three to five years from now. Due to our small size, this level of uncertainty is particularly problematic, because if I guess wrong in making a hiring decision, it will have ramifications for many years. Therefore, I prefer to recruit people who have the capacity to fill varying roles, so that their responsibilities can be fairly easily changed as our business changes. It makes us more flexible.

Speed is a difficult organizational attribute to achieve in the academic world. In my consulting experiences, I have worked with companies that were highly focused on dramatically improving their "speed-to-market" capabilities. Burlington Industries, for example, was working hard on reducing its production cycle time in response to its increasingly demanding customers. But the concept of speed with institutions of higher education is oxymoronic. Almost by definition, universities are slow to respond to changes in their environment. Two of the principal reasons for our tortoise-like movement are shared governance and the risk-averse nature of most faculty. Deans of business schools cannot mandate curriculum changes in degree programs, nor are they empowered to make promotions within the tenure system. We operate under a shared governance system that requires faculty approval of any alterations in the curricula, as well as universitywide approval for creating any new degree programs. Tenure and promotion decisions are made by a faculty committee composed of professors from across the university. The professional schools have their own tenure and promotion committees that "recommend" tenure decisions to the university T&P committee. This does not promote speed.

Several accounting professors at the University of North Carolina had proposed creating a master's in accounting program that would accept students as juniors and have them complete both their B.A. and master's in three years. This would mean that an accounting student would finish in five years with two degrees rather than only getting one degree after four years of college. These accounting faculty members were very active in the national accounting associations, and they knew their profession was heading toward the requirement for increased accounting courses and credentials. At the time the proposal was made to the faculty at the business school in 1982, this was clearly a leading-edge approach. It took 10 years before the new master's in accounting program was approved and ready to accept students. By 1992, this was no longer a leading-edge concept, and the new program struggled mightily to get off the ground. No business can afford to wait 10 years to launch a new product.

Look for ways that you can influence the speed at which your unit responds to its customers and market opportunities. One level of analysis would be to review your decision making processes. How do decisions get made? How fast can you go before you are outrunning your ability to make wise decisions? If you feel the need to review everything before the final product or service is delivered, how does that impact speed?

Another level of analysis worth considering is to review your assumptions about speed to market. In my world, the standard amount of time required to successfully market a new open-enrollment seminar has historically been four to five months from the point of developing the marketing collateral. I had learned this lesson from my first boss in executive education, my peers at other business schools, and my own experiences. The question I have to ask myself now is how appropriate is this standard for today's decision making?

Given the dynamics of the business world today, you have to reexamine all your assumptions that are based on past experience. Can your unit get faster? Yes, I bet it can, but only after you let go of the rules you apply that no longer fit the situation your business is facing today. Realistically challenge every one of those assumptions and you should be able to identify ways to improve your organization's speed.

Speed and flexibility can't happen without an *empowered* work force. The term has become cliché, which erodes its meaning. At one extreme, empowerment has become synonymous with freedom, implying that empowered associates would be free to do things their own way rather than following instructions from someone in authority. At the other extreme, it has come to represent a work force that is fully developed and therefore does not require any direct supervision. The dictionary definition of *empower* is "to give authority or power to" (someone else). Organizations that concentrate power and authority at certain high levels in corporate headquarters are inherently slow and inflexible. Responding quickly to new market opportunities, or adeptly changing direction to combat a new competitive attack, requires authority to act at the field level.

Empowerment can have multiple layers inside business units. Power is different from authority in that it has a much broader connotation. Authority primarily refers to positional power—something that is visible in the organizational chart. There are other sources of power. For example, expert power is based upon an individual's superior technical knowledge—having expertise in a meaningful content area that others do not have adds to your power. Referent power is derived from an individual's charisma. It is reflected in the person's aura—one that exudes powerfulness and leads us to think that this is someone whom we should follow. Arnold Palmer has referent power, for example. Standing by the fairway, attending my first professional golf tournament in 1971, I was watching Palmer walk toward the green. There was a slight drizzle and a chill in the air for early April in North Carolina. He turned to me and said, "Nice day we're having in Greensboro, ain't it?" All I could muster up as a reply was a muffled "Yep," and I'm sure I had that sick smile on my face that you get when you know you are talking with someone who is way out of your league. Palmer has been losing his expert power over the years as his golfing skills diminish, but his personal charisma is as much a force today as it was 30 years ago.

You do not have to give everyone formal authority to make decisions to truly empower your associates. Empowerment to me is more a factor of how willing you are to share power and influence. Table 5.1 illustrates how leaders apply power. As you see from the table, traditionally power was viewed as a zero-sum game—the more you have, the less available for me. If you agree with that point of view, then you will be very unwilling to share power with your associates. An alternative perspective is to view power as an expandable force rather than as finite. There are no defined units of measurement—no way to determine, for example, that there were 100 units of power at work in your organization. Power grows to fill the space in which it exists. If you expand the

T a b l e 5.1

How leaders use/apply power.

Traditional	Empowering
• Power is a zero-sum game	• Power is an expandable pie
• The less power subordinates have, the more you can get them to do what you want	• Keeping people powerless fosters dependence and limits risk taking
• I lose power by giving it	• I gain power by giving it
• People will abuse power and take advantage of the organization	• The more people feel power, the greater their satisfaction (the greater their performance)

space, you increase the amount of power that can be exercised. In this scenario, as the leader, the more power your associates have, the more power available for you.

The types of power you can share with your associates can be aligned with their individual talents. For example, if someone on your staff has technical expertise, you can help him establish power in the organization as a result of what he knows. Alternatively, if one of your associates has very strong interpersonal skills, you can help her leverage those talents to enhance her referent power. One way to increase the power of your colleagues is to publicly recognize them for their accomplishments. If the unit successfully completes a project, why should you receive all the glory? Share the wealth of praise and recognition with your staff and you will enhance their power and influence around the company. This increases your power and influence as well.

It is critically important that you create an atmosphere of *open communications* throughout your unit. Nothing breeds dissension and distrust more than communication blockades. If your associates believe you are keeping information from them, they will assume the information is bad news. If you make it difficult for subordinates to bring you bad news, then you lose the opportunity to solve problems since you won't know they exist. If activities occur in complete isolation from others, then there is likely to be duplication of effort and repetition of the same mistakes. Especially in times of change, there is no substitute for frequent, positive, and candid interactions with people face-to-face. Make sure your associates know all that they need to know in order to perform their responsibilities at the highest level. Do not assume they have information simply because you have it.

Case in point: A large textile company, in the midst of the major changes affecting that industry over the past 20 years, asked me to work with the senior management team of one of the key divisions. During the course of a meeting, Elizabeth, one of the product managers, expressed her frustration with the lack of information she had available to do her job effectively. Elizabeth was the youngest member of the management team and had only been with the company for two years. As a product manager, she was responsible for the profitability of a product line. Yet Elizabeth was not permitted to look at her products' P&Ls. "I am being challenged to increase my profit margins," she said, "and I don't have any idea how much profit we make on my products—nor do I have sufficient information to know how to change it." The two most senior executives in the room responded, trying to be supportive, but also wanting to end Elizabeth's whining. "We can't give you that data," the division controller replied. "If you go to work for one of our competitors, or heaven forbid, one of our customers, they will know our margins and we'll be dead in the water." Not only was the message to Elizabeth that she needed to figure out how to increase profits without having any data on which to base her decisions; but it was also quite clearly communicated that "we don't trust you." Elizabeth quit the company within 18 months of that meeting, and neither the controller nor the division president understood why she left.

On any employee satisfaction survey, poor communications with managers is either number 1 or number 2 on the list of main complaints. On the other hand, you will never be able to communicate enough to satisfy all your associates. But you must take this seriously and do your best to make sure people have the information they need, when they need it, in the form they need it, in order to perform well. Hoarding information is a covert act of exercising power. In order to do your job, you need to come to me to get the information I have. Maybe I'll give it to you and maybe I won't. Sounds childish—and it is childish. Sadly, it is also incredibly common. Go out of your way to let everyone know what's going on in the organization, what you know about initiatives across the company as a whole, and what might be coming up in the near future. Then, make sure that you keep the communications link open to each and every one of your staff members. Invite them to fill you in on their activities, and ask for their input on what they think is working or not working in the unit. Never, ever shoot the messenger who brings you bad news. The first time you do that will be the last time you get bad news in time enough for you to do something about it.

"Thinking outside the box" is such a common expression that it has become a cliché. Yet despite the widespread use of that concept, *innovation* is counterculture in most organizations. Many executives I have met express their concern about the lack of initiative shown by their firm's midlevel managers. Several times I have been asked to develop a program that would teach risk taking. "Our people wait to be told what to do" is a common lament. "They need to have more ownership . . . take more risks." While I have designed programs to enhance creativity and creative thinking, I have to be honest with these potential clients and confess that I don't know how to design a program to develop risk taking. But, I will tell the executives, that is not the problem that you should be addressing. The lack of risk taking in the company is more likely due to problems with the work environment and corporate culture than to risk aversion among employees.

Most people (particularly at the middle levels) want to take risks and try new ways of doing things in organizations, but they have learned not to. If an associate asks you to approve a simple decision he wants to make, or asks you a question to which you know he already has the answer, before you chop his head off for wasting your time, stop to consider why the person has come to you. One reason could be a lack of confidence or, perhaps, a somewhat neurotic need for approval before taking action. My bet, however, is that the individual has learned there is a high price to pay for being wrong in the organization. People don't necessarily have to learn this from personal experience. They learn through both observation and storytelling (oral history). It doesn't take long to figure out how much risk taking the environment will allow.

Perhaps you don't agree with me that most people would take risks if they were encouraged to do so. It is similar to the difference of seeing the glass as being half full or half empty. Douglas McGregor postulated a distinction between Theory X and Theory Y employees over 40 years ago. The Theory X workers, according to McGregor, are those who require close supervision, don't really want to accept responsibility, will take advantage of a situation if given the opportunity, and don't really care about their work. Theory Y employees, on the other hand, want responsibility, seek out new opportunities, enjoy being challenged, and will not abuse power or the freedom associated with it. Clearly there are both Theory X and Theory Y people in the work force.

The question to consider is what are the proportions in your organization—particularly among those in the midlevel managerial ranks? Most companies have far more Theory Y associates than Theory Xers. If that is true, then we do not need to teach them risk taking—they have the natural inclination to take initiative and try new approaches. What is needed is to work on their managers, at the upper-middle to senior levels, to learn how to create an environment where risk taking is encouraged and rewarded. Or more importantly, to help upper-level managers learn how to avoid punishing people for making mistakes.

That is easier said than done, of course. You cannot afford to wait for the company culture to change from one that carries a high price for failure to one that supports and promotes risk taking. Make progress on a microlevel—in your unit—by identifying the local barriers to creativity and innovation. Here is a "top 10" list of specific suggestions that can enhance risk taking and innovation within your corner of the organization:

1. Dedicate time to open discussions about risk taking. Ask your associates under what conditions they feel comfortable taking action without your approval. Ask them what stops them from trying out new ideas. And ask them how they perceive your ability to be innovative.

2. Establish boundaries for their risk taking. Define the limits you will accept as well as the areas in which you want to see them innovate.

3. Create a recognition-reward system for risk taking, regardless of whether the risk taken was successful.

4. Make sure there are frequent debriefings to highlight what has been learned from any new activities. Get the message across that the only way to fail is to fail to learn from a failure. People can learn much more from things that did not work out than from successes.

5. Be open about your failures and mistakes from the past. Help your associates learn what you learned from those experiences and show them that failures are not necessarily career breakers.

6. Make sure you are not the barrier to risk taking. Avoid micromanaging or overly influencing the activities of your associates. You have to give them room to experiment and try methods that you would not attempt.

7. At the same time, you cannot let them go completely on their own. Monitor your associates' risk taking to make sure they are staying within the boundaries and not getting themselves (and your unit) into serious difficulties. In this regard, you must serve as the insulation between your staff and the rest of the organization in order to protect them from the company's culture if it carries a high price for failure.

8. Constantly benchmark your unit with other similar units inside and outside your organization. Be liberal with how you define "similar," and help your associates stretch their minds by analyzing how others tackle problems and issues.

9. Organize an educational experience on creativity and innovation for your staff. Everyone has the capacity to be creative, but most of us have been trained to conform and color within the lines. Help your associates relearn how to tap into their creativity through some training activities.

10. Do not allow your staff to maintain the status quo. Challenge all of your processes to make sure the group is applying the best current thinking for solving business problems.

CREATING A LEARNING-ORIENTED CULTURE

Fostering innovation and risk taking is intertwined with the managerial leader's role in creating a learning-oriented culture inside the unit. If you do not manage the learning process in your organization, the ways in which the associates learn will be haphazard and independent. This result is slow and imprecise—there is no system in place to help everyone share knowledge gained, nor is there any managed focus on what is being learned. The expression "Work smarter, not harder" is worthy of consideration (although my version is "Work wiser, not harder"). It is very important to optimize organizational learning when coping with a rapidly changing, highly competitive business environment. No company can afford to wait for everyone to climb the learning curve independently. It is the era of the knowledge economy. Those organizations that can rapidly expand their knowledge, and put their learning to use effectively, will have a significant competitive advantage. There are several dimensions to thinking about how you can best manage organizational learning.

Consider the Myriad Ways
Knowledge Can Enter the Organization

Hiring associates with varied backgrounds and experiences is one way to bring in more knowledge. Educational programs and conferences are also vehicles for adding knowledge to the company. Competitive intelligence, the act of systematically collecting information about your industry and key competitors, brings important new knowledge into the organization. Market research, customer satisfaction surveys, and industry association reports are other resources that contain important knowledge to collect. Your job is to make sure you tap into as many sources of knowledge as possible that have relevance to your unit's activities. Again, be liberal in your definition of what is relevant—use sources that are nontraditional. Don't just look in the same places as everybody else.

Create a Systematic Approach to Disseminating the Knowledge Gained

This is not a time to rely on the grapevine. Knowledge that is not shared with the right people does little good. For example, if you learned something while attending a professional conference, what would you do with that information? If you are like most people, you will file the tidbit in your memory and hope you can recall it when you need it. Of course, you will more likely lose that piece of knowledge than be able to retrieve it from your memory. It's not a very effective or efficient system, given all that we have to think about these days. Instead, you could write a quick message to yourself that could also be copied to a few others whom you thought could benefit from this information. Then, your message could be electronically filed and retrieved on demand. That's just one small way you can enhance organizational learning.

Use the Knowledge That Has Been Gained to Make Better Decisions

The systematic collection and dissemination of new knowledge will not help your organization at all if that information isn't used to make more fact-based decisions. Encourage your associates to apply what they have learned. Reward them when they do, and hold them accountable for making mistakes they made before when they don't demonstrate learning.

A critical part of transforming the organization's culture is to make sure there is sufficient *focus on human resource development*. The famous quote from Roger Milliken frames this best: "Insanity is doing things the same way and expecting different results." If you are striving for significant changes in the ways in which the organization operates, then there must be changes in the ways in which the people inside the organization operate. There are two options for how to make this happen. Either you can fire everybody and hire an entirely new set of employees (which will ensure that things will be done differently), or you can spend time, effort, and funds on developing the current employees to have the new skill sets that are required. Simply proclaiming that from now on the organization will operate differently will not make it happen. Since you will not be firing everyone, the only viable option is to focus on development. In this regard, you should think carefully about the competencies your associates will need to demonstrate in order to succeed in the new organization. Once you are able to identify the new skills, knowledge, and abilities that will be required, you can work out ways to build these capabilities among your associates. In essence, you will create individual development plans for each of your staff members by assessing their current capabilities in comparison with the new set of competencies. There may be some knowledge gaps that are similar among many of your associates. In those instances, a customized executive educational activity may be the best way to close the gap.

Case in point: A utility company determined that its managers were not effective collaborators inside the organization. These were people who were trained to be competitive negotiators with customers and suppliers and who used similar approaches when working with their colleagues across business units and divisional lines. This situation was creating a lot of ill will within the organization and was manifested by internal warfare. I was involved in designing a two-day program on collaborative problem solving that focused on building the skill sets for achieving win-win results with internal conflicts. The customized program was conducted frequently in order to reach a large number of managers in a relatively short time. By addressing development in this way, the company was able to create a common foundation for midlevel managers to improve internal collaboration. The objective was to change the culture, not to develop just a few people.

For individuals who have gaps between their current set of capabilities and the identified new set of competencies, there are several alternatives for development. Certainly, some new skills can be obtained from other educational activities. However, most new competencies are best developed through on-the-job experiences. Job rotations, involvement in task forces for companywide initiatives, short-term projects, and overseas assignments are all methods for developing the new competencies required for success.

Creating a *lean* organization was one of the descriptors my clients identified for the ideal company. While this mostly has connotations for the organization as a whole, there are ways in which managerial leaders can make contributions to "leanness." The most obvious way is to be careful to avoid overstaffing. It is not uncommon to hear associates point to inadequate staffing as the reason behind poor performance—"if we only had more people, then we wouldn't have these problems." There are times when that statement is undoubtedly correct, but there are likely more times when it is inaccurate. Before you add people, make sure that it is truly an issue of insufficient staffing as opposed to process or people problems.

Another way to stay lean is the judicious use of temporary employees. In the early nineties, contract employment became a popular vehicle for avoiding paying the benefits and fringes required for permanent hires. It got to the point in many firms where the overutilization of temporary associates led to serious quality concerns. You should not expect to get the same level of commitment to quality and customer service from contract employees as you do from permanent staff members. The less loyalty the company demonstrates to its employees, the less loyalty it will receive in return. And less loyalty was the result of the wide-scale use of temporary workers where there was no real difference between the work required of them and the work required of the permanent employees. In addition, it generated a fair amount of discontent. However, the occasional use of contract employment makes sense in today's environment. Adding permanent positions to address growth when there is no guarantee the organization's growth will continue does not add to the organization's flexibility. If possible, hire temporary associates to cover new staffing needs for growth spurts until you can better determine the stability of customer demand. If the growth is continuous and relatively secure, then you can change the new positions to permanent ones. If the continued growth is uncertain, you will not be saddled with excessive overhead. We employed this approach at Emory University when we were building up the executive education portfolio. We did not have sufficient staff to cover all the new programs we were planning to roll out; yet it was difficult to predict how successful we were going to be in gaining enrollments across the new portfolio, especially in the area of ebusiness. Therefore, we hired several contract employees to serve as program managers on a project-by-project basis. These were individuals who came through referrals, who were experienced but did not want to have full-time positions, and whom we were easily able to train to handle the responsibilities. The most important lesson I learned from this staffing option was to treat the contract employees with the same respect as the permanent staff—and to make sure everyone else acted similarly. We made sure they were invited to staff meetings, office celebrations, and planning sessions, but no ill will was created if they chose not to participate.

My final word of advice on maintaining a lean organization is to be careful with your expenditures. The relative ease of keeping close tabs on the budget is heavily dependent upon the size of your unit, the diversity of its activities, and your managerial style. If you are fortunate to be working with primarily Theory Y associates, all that you need to do is to help them understand that conservation of financial resources is good for the business. They have the capacity to react as if it is their money on the line, and so they will be careful with how they spend it. If you are not this fortunate, and have more Theory X employees, then it is best not to delegate the budget control to anyone else in your unit. You may have someone else handle the data entry and reconciliations, but you should monitor your expenditures frequently. Even in an organization that seemingly tolerates overspending budget lines, you would be wise to end the fiscal year with some dollars left over. Demonstrating your ability to conserve resources will make you much more likely to get more when you truly need it—and this is important to the future progress of your unit.

As change is a constant in business, all organizations need effective change agents throughout the enterprise. The more you can demonstrate your openness to change and your ability to lead others through change, the more you will distinguish yourself from other managers in the company. The next step in this endeavor is to help make sure that the associates who work for you are being developed to their fullest potential, which is the focus of Part Two.

QUESTIONS AND EXERCISES

- Determine if there are other managers at your level in the organization who share the drive to influence significant change in the company. Hold informal discussions with them to identify ways in which you could assist one another.
- Deepen your understanding of the reasons why the managers and executives above you may be resistant to change. If you cannot talk to your direct supervisor about this topic, find others at that level who would be willing to speak candidly with you about the organization's culture.
- Are you aware of any innovations in the company that were the result of a midlevel manager's efforts? Look for best practices inside the organization—see if you can talk with people who have been successful at driving change without having the formal authority of senior-level managers.

PART TWO

DEVELOPING YOUR ASSOCIATES AND YOURSELF

CHAPTER 6

Leadership Competencies

"My people and I have come to an agreement which satisfies us both. They are to say what they please, and I am to do what I please."

—Frederick the Great

Enabling your associates to work at their very best is at the core of managerial leadership. Note that selection of the word *enabling* is purposeful—"making able; making it possible for"—as leadership today is so much more about creating environments where people can succeed than it is about making decisions or getting things done individually. You cannot possibly handle by yourself everything that must be done. Nor are most managers in situations where they are capable of making all decisions themselves and simply dictating actions to their subordinates. That is just too slow and nonempowering for organizations to function effectively.

The solution lies in leadership development. In its broadest context, development relates to enabling the individual to grow in skills, knowledge, and abilities to perform at his or her highest possible level now and for the future. I cannot imagine an organization that does not need to have its people performing at their most "effective state." Yet the area of human resource development is one of the least understood, and one of the lowest priorities, in most companies with which I have worked. It doesn't make sense.

The leadership challenge is to find ways to make sure your associates are being developed regardless of whether the company has a vibrant human resource development function. The critical ingredients to consider are:

- Creating an environment where associates are encouraged to learn and grow
- Identifying the most important competencies that associates must develop
- Providing the mechanisms for associates to develop those competencies
- Generating individual development plans for associates based on their unique sets of skills and deficiencies
- Integrating development into the day-to-day activities as much as possible

The issue of creating an environment that supports associate development has already been covered. The only point worth adding is that you need to frequently reinforce your encouragement and support. This is especially important in an organization that is highly focused on getting results and hitting its numbers. When push comes to shove, the concern for people development gets significantly downplayed.

Several years ago, the Fluor Daniel Corporation created People Development Boards in each of its business units to highlight the importance of human resource development across the board. It was a pioneering organizational structure to promote development among associates at all levels. Then the company's financial performance fell well below expectations and its share price fell precipitously. This resulted in a change in leadership at the top and a greatly increased sense of uncertainty throughout the organization. Guess what happened to the focus on development?

It is understandable that in times of organizational duress, "peripheral" activities get cut or, at the very least, downplayed. But it is precisely in times of duress when human resource development is of utmost importance. Be aware, as a managerial leader, that these periods of organizational stress provide incredible opportunities for development and growth among associates. Despite any cutbacks that the company may exercise in development, make sure you don't lose focus. You may need to be more creative in how you enable your associates to grow, but you do not need to stop helping them develop.

IDENTIFYING THE KEY COMPETENCIES

It is not sufficient to simply create a supportive environment for human resource development. Given the perennial lack of resources and time to let development happen at its own pace, you need to concentrate the development activities in those areas that are of highest priority to the corporation. This is not a new concept —just one that is often overlooked or given little attention. Several decades ago, human resource managers used the expression ksa's to describe the priority areas for human resource development— "knowledge, skills, and abilities." The word *competencies* became popular several years ago as a way of creating some focus for development efforts. It remains the favored expression today, but it is not much different from ksa's. The point is that an organization should identify the set of competencies its people should be able to effectively demonstrate in order to provide a road map for human resource development initiatives. These competencies will likely differ across layers and levels of the organization—perhaps across business units as well. The competencies should have an orientation toward the future—what skills do our managers need to demonstrate five years from now to make our company successful —since it will take time to develop those competencies. If you only focus on skill sets required right now, by the time they are effectively developed they may be obsolete, or of far less importance than some other competencies that should have been anticipated.

Many companies have generated competency lists to assist them in focusing their human resource development efforts. The sophistication level runs quite a range from somewhat elementary one-line statements to highly elaborate competency maps. It is important to be careful in identifying the competencies since they will serve as the blueprint for development activities. But it is not very difficult to accomplish. I have seen many such competency lists, and the ones focused on management and leadership contain similar elements. Many times, it is the process of determining the competencies that is more important than the end product.

Case in point: A colleague of mine—Professor David Schweiger—and I were hired by the Robert Bosch Corporation (US) in 1995 to help the company develop the managerial competencies that would be required of its middle managers 20 years out (2015) so it could align its human resource development initiatives accordingly. No American firm thinks in terms of 20 years from now (at best, it would be 20 months), but this U.S. division of the huge German Bosch Corporation was interested in addressing its long-term sustainability. A task force had been created representing line and staff functions, led by Thomas Heinz, a German human resources manager serving a two-year rotation in the States. Thomas was an exceptionally capable human resources professional but knew that the task force needed some outside help in generating the competencies. The task force's initial cut at it was primarily a list of personal traits that would be appropriate for effective midlevel managers. We helped members of the task force to look at the competencies from a more behavioral perspective— determining what the midlevel managers should be able to do as opposed to what they should be like as individuals. Through a series of focus groups, intensive interviews with their senior executives, and benchmarking research with relevant, best-practice companies, we were able to assist the task force in identifying nine key managerial competencies, shown in Table 6.1.

In reviewing these nine competencies, you may be struck by the force of the obvious. You could conclude that we could have just as easily generated the list without the need or the expense of the interviews. What you don't know is that behind each of the competencies was a more detailed mapping of the associated behaviors that were much more thorough for Bosch. Those were proprietary and thus cannot be shared in this publication. But there is a lot of truth to the "blinding case of the obvious" criticism. The competencies themselves were not difficult to determine. They are consistent with many other firms' lists. What made this a successful endeavor was the fact that many people were brought into the process and the competencies were developed truly from "within" —from the opinions and perspectives of managers inside Bosch. As consultants, Dave Schweiger and I simply created the framework for the process and provided the behavioral definitions behind the

T a b l e   6.1

Managerial leadership competentcies—Robert Bosch US.

BOSCH
Each competency and its definition are as follows:

- **Promote Personal and Associate Development and Empowerment**—Help self and associates to continually learn, improve performance, acquire new competencies, and take additional initiative and responsibilities.
- **Encourage Risk Taking, Innovation, and Organizational Development**—Cultivate the development and free flow of ideas and initiatives that work processes, technologies, products, and/or services.
- **Build Partnerships with External Customers**—Build a relationship with customers to understand their current and future needs and expectations and solicit feedback on how well Bosch is meeting them and be more effective in meeting them.
- **Demonstrate Socially Responsive and Ethical Behavior**—Understand and integrate into decisions and behaviors important legal, ethical, and social considerations.
- **Solve Problems and Make Decisions**—Prioritize a variety of complex problems and decisions and effectively resolve and implement them in a timely manner.
- **Build and Utilize Internal Networks and Teams**—Take initiative to build and utilize internal networks and teams throughout the worldwide Bosch organization to facilitate organization performance.
- **Engage Strategic Thinking**—Consider and integrate into decisions the long-range, organizationwide impact that the decisions might have.
- **Communicate with Others**—Demonstrate effective two-way communication strategies and techniques to facilitate work effectiveness, goal achievement, and employee motivation.
- **Understanding RBUS International Organization, Business, and Industry**—Understanding Bosch's internal and external international environment, vision, mission, strategies, and goals.

---

competencies. From this list, we helped Thomas Heinz build a comprehensive matrix that incorporated both educational and on-the-job activities as a road map for competency development. The goal was for each manager to have a competency handbook that would serve as the key resource for determining individualized development plans for his associates. The initial buy-in from the managers was quite high—due much more to the process we utilized than the end product that was generated.

The competency project with Bosch taught me many lessons. One of those key lessons was that the identification of a solid list of competencies doesn't accomplish anything if managers in the organization fail to use them as guides for development. It is true, however unfair, that the human resources department should not develop the competency list by itself. Line managers will not accept the list of competencies unless it comes from the managers themselves. If you want to work on competency identification for your own unit, seek the assistance of HR but make sure that your associates and senior managers provide the bulk of the input.

DEVELOPING THE COMPETENCIES

With competencies in hand, you can generate individualized development plans for each of your associates. Think broadly about the range of activities that would be developmental. Certainly, outside of your company's own training classes, there are executive education programs available throughout the United States. At Goizueta Business School (Emory University), for example, seminars are offered in marketing, finance, ebusiness, leadership, and general management. One important advantage to participating in these open-enrollment executive education programs is the opportunity to interact with managers from a range of different companies and industries. Your associates can learn as much from their peers as from the instructors.

Another option is to develop a customized program tailored to meet the specific needs of your organization. While the participants lose the opportunity to learn from managers in other companies, they gain by having a more precise focus on the educational activity that is directly relevant to their situation. Custom programs are effective in establishing a common foundation or framework for addressing a set of business issues across the boundaries of an organization. They are also excellent vehicles for expanding the development of internal networks within complex companies.

Case in point: Burlington Industries, the global textile company, was a client during my time as a faculty member at the University of North Carolina. The firm was just seeing the light at the end of a long tunnel due to a leveraged buyout that was its defense of a hostile takeover attempt. Burlington was fighting significant debt payments from the LBO and was not able to address any other long-term activities until it came out from under that weight. In 1992, with much of the debt behind it, Burlington wanted to develop a customized executive education program for its highest-potential middle managers—the people identified in the company's succession planning as the next generation of senior leaders of the company. Because of the LBO, Burlington had sold off some pretty big pieces of the company and was left with eight business units that operated mostly independently. By 1992, the company's leadership knew that Burlington needed to function more as one company than as eight completely separate firms. The executive program enabled the company to greatly expand the business knowledge among this next generation of leadership and create a network of peers at this level across the business units. As we worked with the participants in the classroom activities, it was fascinating to watch them realize how much they could learn from, and help, each other. This level of appreciation for leveraging their capabilities across the businesses was not something that could have been dictated from above. It was something that had to come from the group itself—and the results were impressive.

These forms of classroom education represent just a few slices of the pie for competency development. Much larger pieces are represented by on-the-job experiences. The competency development matrixes that were produced for the Bosch Corporation included both elements: educational programs and on-the-job experiences (see Tables 6.2 and 6.3). In addition to task completion, development of the individual should be a factor in the decision making process of making job and project assignments for your associates. For example, international rotations are critically important in global companies—especially at the early stages of a manager's career. Regardless of whether or not the individual will have direct international responsibilities, anyone with significant managerial responsibilities in a global organization needs to be exposed to living and working abroad. By having younger managers experience international assignments, the company gets a lot more leverage from what the managers have learned, as they will potentially work many more years in the organization. It is also a lot eas-

T a b l e   6.2

Competency development matrix—educational activities.

Competency Development Matrix—Educational Activities   BOSCH

COMPETENCIES

Formal Education Topic Area	1 Personal Develop.	2 Risk Taking	3 Customers	4 Ethics	5 Problem Solving	6 Networks	7 Strategies	8 Comm.	9 Business
Business Benchmarking		P	S						S
Business law—German & U.S.				P		S			
Change Management		S		S					
Coaching & Feedback (Managing Performance)	P	S			S		P		
Communications	S	P	S			P		P	
Continuous Improvement		P		P					
Delegate & Empower	P	S		S					
Ethics/Values/Vision				P		S			S
Finance		S					S		P
General Management	S	S	S	S	P	S	S P	P	P
High Performance Teams						P			
Influence & Collaborative Negotiations			P		P			P	
Innovation & Creativity		P		S			S		
Interaction Skills: Building Slef-Esteem	P								
International Business—Finance,Mktg., Oper.				S		P	S	S	P
Labor Relations						S		S	
Leadership (Feedback Driven)	P			S		S			
Managing Diverse Work Force						P		S	
Managing Stress	S								
Managing Time & Priorities	S				P				
Manufacturing					S		P		
Marketing			S		P				
Problem Solving					P				
Project Management					P				
Quality Operations			P		P		S		
Speed to Market		S		S					P
Strategic Management							P		P

P = Primary topic for developing competency   S= Secondary topic for developing competency

Table 6.3

Competency development matrix—on-the-job experiences.

BOSCH

Introduction

Besides formal education, there are "on-the-job managerial activities" that can enhance the development of managerial competencies. They should become an integral part of your associate development plan. In this part of the catalogue, such activities are described. Experiences occur in one of two ways in organizations: a) each of us learns by doing his/her normal job; b) by organizing patterns of activities specific opportunities for learning can be created.

With the identification of the managerial competencies, it is now possible for us to use the second approach more systematically and effectively. It is the purpose of this section to focus on this approach and to illustrate the possible types of activities that can be structured and the competencies they are lost likely to develop.

In the following section you will find a matrix which illustrates the relationship between the activities and the competencies to which they specifically relate. Following the matrix is a description of each of the major activities.

COMPETENCIES

Development Activities	1 Personal Develop.	2 Risk Taking	3 Customer	4 Ethics	5 Problem Solving	6 Network	7 Strategy	8 Comm.	9 Business
Managing Challenging Situations	P	P	S	P	P	S	P	P	S
Job Rotation	P	S	P	P*	S	P	S	P	P
Job Exchange	P	P	S	P*	S	P	S	P	P
Special Team Projects	P	P	S	S	P	P	P	P	S
Mentoring	P	S	S	P	P	P	S	P	P
Nontraditional Roles	P	S	S	S	P	P	S	P	S
Teaching/Training	P	S	S	S	S	S	S	P	S
Orientation	S	S	S	S	S	P	S	S	P
Training Assignment	S	S	S	S	S	P	S	S	P

*Cross-country rotations   P= Primary topic for developing competency   S= Secondary topic for developing competency

87

ier to send them abroad than older managers, who tend to be more expensive to expatriate, have more family issues, and have less energy for such activities. Other job-related developmental activities include serving on special project or task force teams, rotating into different functional areas or business units, being put in turn-around (firefighting) situations, and serving a rotation in training and development. You learn a great deal if you are in a position where you have to teach others!

Determining the best possible combination of developmental activities is especially critical for your most talented associates—the people you don't want to lose. Typically, these high potentials are thirsty for new and different experiences. They want to develop their capabilities, and they expect the company to find ways to support their growth. A combination of educational and job-related development activities provides a well-rounded approach. Education by itself lacks the learning that would be gained from application. On-the-job experiences lack the focus of intensive education and are too slow without the turbo boosts from educational programs.

Your responsibility in this process is to create individual development plans for each of your associates, focusing on the competencies of greatest relevance to the organization and utilizing both training and job-related developmental vehicles. This is best achieved through ongoing one-on-one dialogs to ensure that the associate is an active player in the process. Ultimately, each associate is responsible for his or her own development. Your role, as manager, is to guide, encourage, and enable the associates to develop themselves.

To be an effective managerial leader, you need to be skilled in the three components of developing people: coaching, teaching, and mentoring. As a coach, you are zeroing in on results and developing your associates' performance capabilities. As a teacher, you are concentrating on helping them to learn and apply new knowledge or skills they acquire. As a mentor, you are focusing on their longer-term career and personal development. While these are not independent activities, they have different implications for leadership practices and thus warrant separate consideration. The ability to serve associates as an effective coach, teacher, and mentor is the hallmark of great leadership from within the managerial ranks. The following chapters explore each of these areas in more depth to help you consider how to enhance your capabilities across the three dimensions.

QUESTIONS AND EXERCISES

- Create a competency map for your top associates. What are the critical skills, abilities, or knowledge they must demonstrate now in order to be most successful?
- Determine educational activities that would most help your high-potential managers develop these competencies. What educational resources are available to them?
- Identify some nontraditional on-the-job experiences that could be utilized to build the competencies in your key people. What types of special assignments or projects could be developed to enhance the business and develop your people at the same time?

CHAPTER 7

Coaching

"Once more unto the breach, dear friends,
*   once more;*
Or close the wall up with our English dead!
In peace there's nothing so becomes a man
As modest stillness and humility;
But when the blast of war blows in our ears,
Then imitate the action of the tiger."
—William Shakespeare, *King Henry V*

Executive and managerial coaching has become a big business. A number of leading companies, such as General Electric, Cox Enterprises, and The Home Depot, have made extensive use of outside coaches for their managers. Firms that specialize in management coaching are popping up everywhere. Many industrial psychologists have incorporated coaching into their service offerings. I have learned much about the movement through my colleague at Emory University, Rick Gilkey, who is writing a book on executive coaching with consultant Randy White, formerly with the Center for Creative Leadership.

The use of outside coaches has some distinct advantages for companies, particularly if their internal capacity for coaching is underdeveloped. But outside coaching should not be viewed as a substitute for the coaching role that managers must play for their direct reports. The two are somewhat complementary in that to be an effective coach, it is helpful to gain the insight from also being coached by someone else. From the perspective of enhancing your managerial leadership, the focus of this chapter is on the challenges of coaching your own people rather than on the pros and cons of utilizing outside coaches for selected individuals.

LESSONS FROM ATHLETICS

When thinking about coaching, the image that most naturally comes to mind is an athletic coach. Consider a set of responsibilities for the coach of a basketball team, for example. They include:

- Analyze the competition and determine strategies to defeat them.
- Recruit, retain, develop talent.
- Build teamwork to create synergy and optimize performance.
- Help each team member to understand his or her role(s) to contribute to team success.
- Make sure the team, and the individual players, continually improves its performance.

The coach's bottom line is the overall won-lost record, with particular emphasis on victories in the most important games. In other words, the job of the coach is to get results through others. Players are the ones who execute, not coaches. But if the team is unsuccessful, the coach is the one held most accountable. You cannot get rid of all the players when the team is not performing, but you can fire the coach.

A great coach gets the best possible performance out of his or her players and does so consistently over the long term as experienced team members leave and new ones come on board. Legendary coaches have impressive won-lost records but also demonstrate other qualities that make them stand out from their peers. There are myriad lists one can come up with regarding what makes for a legendary coach in athletics—these are the qualities that make my top 10:

1. Understands the game exceptionally well
2. Has a keen eye for talent, especially talent that is underdeveloped
3. Motivates and inspires the players on an ongoing basis
4. Assigns roles that get the most out of each team member
5. Develops the team to perform at a higher level than the sum of its potential talent

6. Builds confidence among the team members in their abilities to succeed

7. Makes effective tactical decisions during the game as adjustments to the strategy

8. Runs highly effective practices to improve team performance

9. Develops meaningful relationships and establishes trust with the individual players

10. Operates under a strong value system—is fair and consistent

While this list captures the points that strike me as most important, if you pushed me to add one more, it would be the ability to put the game in perspective so as not to take things too seriously.

These qualities have direct application to coaching in the work environment. It is important for a managerial leader to have solid industry knowledge and to be able to identify the talents that people have. Working down these 10 items, the only one that may not fit that well at first glance is running effective practices. There is not much opportunity to practice in the business world (at least not in the traditional sense of the term). Yet it is important that associates constantly learn from their day-to-day activities to enhance team performance as well as to develop their own capabilities. If you think about organizations and individuals that perform at high levels outside of the business world, symphony orchestras come to mind. The musicians in an orchestra spend at least 90 percent of their time practicing—individually, in small sections, and as a full orchestra. No wonder they consistently perform well.

This concept is very important to bring into the workplace—but it requires a much broader view of what constitutes "practice." For example, I asked my staff to conduct regular program debriefings after each rendition of a major executive education seminar. Those involved in the program, from marketing through operations, discussed the things that worked well, those that went wrong, and ways to improve performance for the next session. In this context, each program served as practice for the ones to follow.

Look for ways in which you can bring the concept of practice into your unit. Keep in mind that every job or project has a learning curve associated with it—it takes time for someone to develop his or her capabilities, so do not expect to have an associate perform at the highest level right away. We cannot rely on the chance that through normal day-to-day experiences people will quickly move up that learning curve. Effective coaching combined with quality will dramatically reduce the time needed to climb.

I do not know of anyone who understood the value of effective practice better than Dean Smith, former men's basketball coach at the University of North Carolina. Occasionally, I was able to get his approval to allow a group of executives to watch one of the team's closed practices. While it was a special treat to see a Tar Heel practice for the executives interested in college basketball, there was a learning objective for this activity. The executives could quickly tell why the UNC basketball team was consistently ranked in the nation's top 10 from watching even just a few minutes of a Dean Smith practice. It wasn't due to the amount of time the players spent on the court because UNC was reported to have among the shortest practice sessions in collegiate basketball. What impressed the observers was the structure that Coach Smith employed—his coaching system, if you will. Some examples. There was no excess talking by anyone. Each assistant coach had a role to play in the teaching phases of the practice sessions. The team was divided into smaller groups that rotated through the assistant coaches' stations. When Smith had a point to make, he blew his whistle and everyone ran to him to listen. He would talk to them briefly and send them back to their practice stations. There were set times for water breaks—seniors went first, and the team members worked their way down to the freshmen (even when Michael Jordan was a freshman, he received no special treatment). When the team scrimmaged, it was clear that everyone was there to learn, not to show off. The subs were assigned the roles of playing like the next opposing team so the practice simulated the real game coming up. Again, there were frequent stoppages of play for Coach Smith to teach during the scrimmage.

This structured approach to the way the team learned and practiced built consistency in performance. Some have been critical of Smith's system, believing that it served to constrain the performance of some of his most talented players. And, in fact, some even made a joke about this: "Who is the only man able to keep Michael Jordan from scoring over 20 points a game? Answer: Dean Smith."

But if you measure success by sustained outstanding performance over a significant period of time, Coach Smith's system was incredibly successful. His teams set records for consistency in making the NCAA tournament and for consecutive years in finishing in the top three of the Atlantic Coast Conference, and he has more victories than any other coach in NCAA basketball history. The caliber of the talent Smith was able to recruit to UNC certainly played a major role in his sustained success, but those practices were every bit as critical as the players were to the team's consistent high performance during his tenure as head coach.

I have learned other managerial lessons about coaching from Dean Smith. This is not meant to imply that he is the only outstanding athletic coach who can serve as a model for managerial leaders. It's just that Smith has been someone whom I have been able to observe directly and who has been inspirational to me.

First and foremost, he is a values-driven coach. In his autobiography, *A Coach's Life*, Smith writes about the strong sense of values instilled in him by his parents. It served as the foundation for his coaching—a definite work ethic, the importance of education, a focus on team success, humility, respect for all types of people, and competitiveness. Smith recruited the first African-American player at UNC, Charlie Scott, and helped him survive the challenges that come with fighting racism in the South. Smith was also one of the key supporters of integration in Chapel Hill at the time of desegregation. He built relationships with his players, assistant coaches, and team managers that transcended the basketball court. To this day, many of Smith's former players seek his advice and counsel. There is a standing golf game in June with his former assistant coaches, and Smith has helped a number of the team managers with their careers in business.

It impressed me that during a fund-raising campaign at the university, Coach Smith made a substantial donation to the library, not to athletic scholarships. He made it clear that the primary mission of the university was education, not basketball. It was not by chance that the graduation rate among the basketball players was extraordinarily high under his leadership—upwards of 97 percent.

Even those special players who left UNC before their senior year to enter the NBA draft (James Worthy, Michael Jordan, Jerry Stackhouse, Antawn Jamison, and Vince Carter) all put special clauses in their professional contracts that incorporated graduating from UNC.

Dean Smith was an innovator in the game of basketball. His "four corners" offense was a creative and highly effective end-game strategy that changed college basketball until the shot clock was instituted. Some of Smith's other innovations included devising a half-court defensive press (called run and jump), having the team huddle to set offense-defense just before free throws, and having a player who made a basket thank the teammate who passed him the ball that made the goal possible. When the three-point basket was first being considered in college basketball, representing a revolutionary change in the game, Smith was an advocate. Normally, one might expect a successful coach to resist a dramatic change in the game and would work hard to maintain the status quo in order to maintain his competitive advantage. But Smith saw the value in making this major change in the game itself, and he quickly adapted and learned how to alter his strategy on both offense and defense accordingly.

In the management world, the key lessons from Dean Smith begin with his operating from a strong set of values and principles. He "walked the talk" by backing up the espoused principles through his actions. Smith showed respect for all individuals and valued diversity. He was able to develop a personal relationship with each of his players that transcended the current work situation. Smith created a dynamic environment that motivated his players as he encouraged innovation and was open to change. He utilized a system of practice that helped his players learn and develop their talents to their fullest potential. Many of the UNC athletes who went on to the NBA were better pros than expected because they had learned to be complete team players. He was fair in how he treated his players, regardless of their ability level. And Smith was consistent in communicating that being in college was all about education. He wanted to see his players receive their degrees and be able to have a career outside of basketball.

COACHING AS A MANAGER

This formula for coaching certainly works in the business context. The caring for each team member—current and former players— should be at the heart of anyone's coaching philosophy. People want to feel that their interests are important and that they are more than simply vehicles for achieving organizational results. As with Dean Smith, industry knowledge, respect for the individual, and an effective system for developing talent are important coaching attributes.

One significant difference between athletic coaching and managerial coaching is the level of attention paid to it. Coaches of athletic teams are totally focused on that responsibility. Coaching is what they do for a living. It is not an additional task being asked of them that is loaded on top of lots of other responsibilities. In the business world, the importance of the coaching role of managers is a relatively new phenomenon. It has always been needed, but only recently have companies begun to understand its importance. Of course, other responsibilities have not been taken away in order to make time for coaching. Therefore, an important challenge you face as a manager is to find the time to be an effective coach. I know of only one way to attack that challenge. You must adjust your view of your managerial role as primarily one of being a coach. Your job is to achieve business results by enabling your associates to perform to their fullest potential both as individuals and as a unit. It is no different from being a basketball coach. The top 10 list of effective coaching in athletics mentioned earlier in the chapter is directly applicable to your coaching as a managerial leader. Therefore, coaching is your primary focus and is built into all your day-to-day activities. You must take advantage of every opportunity to coach— working either with individuals or with the team as a whole.

Surround yourself with competent "assistant coaches"—experienced people who work with subsets of your organization and help you handle the full set of coaching tasks. Many successful athletic coaches prefer to use former players as their assistant coaches. There is nothing wrong with that except you need to be careful to avoid being too inbred. Dean Smith hired one of his former coaches from his days as a player to be an assistant coach—using a mentor to help him run the team. Many of his assistants were not former players but people who brought other skills to the team. The combination worked well for him. Serving in the role of an assistant coach is, in and of itself, a development opportunity. The best way to prepare someone to be a head coach is to mentor him or her through the assistant coach role(s). Within your organization, you can establish these assistant coach positions by altering the job responsibilities of some carefully selected associates. For example, have them take on a project, such as improving work processes, or ask them to serve as mentors for new hires. But do not just throw them into these types of assignments without some preparation. Train them on coaching techniques and what it means to be a managerial coach inside your company. Check in with them periodically to see how they are doing in this role and, most of all, keep coaching them.

MOTIVATING ASSOCIATES

The motivational aspect of effective coaching is highly visible in the athletic world due to the existence of specific games or events. There is a tangible, short-term activity the coach can use to focus the athlete's attention—getting "up for the game," so to speak. Motivating performance in these clearly identifiable activities does not translate that readily into the business context. A manager is not about to hold pregame pep talks every few days. Yet, utilizing an athletic coach's motivational techniques must be popular with managers, as evidenced by the number of successful coaches who have written business-oriented leadership books (Rick Pitino, Pat Riley, and Joe Torre, to name a few).

Intuitively, we know there is a strong connection between employee motivation and performance. Much of the research in this area has focused more on the relationship between satisfaction and motivation—the hypothesis being that the more satisfied the employee, the higher his or her motivation. From that point, we make the inference that the higher the employee's motivation, the stronger his or her performance. Given the fact that associates need to be constantly motivated to perform their daily responsibilities, it would make sense to apply motivational models different from those in the sports world. Thus, the popular books by athletic coaches have less applicability than the classic writings of researchers who studied motivation and job satisfaction in the workplace. The pioneering studies of motivation from the mid-1900s by Maslow, Herzberg, and Adams continue to have relevance for today's work force. It is well worth the time to reexamine their three models, particularly as they pertain to managerial coaching.

Maslow's hierarchy-of-needs model, briefly discussed in Chapter 1, was grounded in psychology. His premise was that people are motivated to satisfy needs at different levels, and they do so in sequence from basic needs (food, clothing, and shelter) to abstract needs (self-actualization). Individuals will not be motivated to address their higher-level needs if they have not first satisfied their needs for basic survival and security. Maslow's contention was that the sequence could not be altered. Thus, people must first satisfy the lower-level needs before they can hope to achieve self-actualization (similar in scope to Goleman's EQ component of self-awareness).

The structured nature of the sequence in Maslow's model has important coaching implications. To build or maintain an associate's motivation, you need to first consider that person's degree of satisfaction with the lower-level needs. The situation that was cited in Chapter 4 about the Medical University of South Carolina offers an illustration of this point. Managers were trying (unsuccessfully) to motivate the MUSC employees to work in interdisciplinary teams while the rumors were flying about Columbia HCA's proposal to acquire the hospital. The employees were concerned about losing their jobs and how they would provide for their families if the merger occurred. They could not be motivated to address the higher-level need of teamwork until they were sufficiently satisfied about their job security. That is why the management team had to first communicate openly about the merger before the team could push for the changes in work processes.

Herzberg's model of motivation built on Maslow's theory, especially regarding the drive to satisfy needs. Herzberg was more the industrial psychologist, and so his perspective was derived directly from the business arena. He determined that there were two distinct categories of motivation in the workplace that addressed satisfaction (see Table 7.1). (A key difference from Maslow's model was that Herzberg did not see those two categories as sequenced, but rather as interactive.) He labeled the first category "hygienic factors." These were elements that could only lead to dissatisfaction for workers, and thus were not considered truly motivational. Job security, company policies and regulations, relationships with other workers, and the work surroundings (facilities) were examples of his hygienic factors. According to Herzberg, the best a manager could do for employees along this category would be to neutralize these factors to avoid dissatisfaction and demotivation. In other words, an attractive office location will not motivate an employee to perform at a high level. At best, it is a neutral item. However, a very unattractive office location can demotivate an employee due to the high level of dissatisfaction it creates.

The other category, called "motivating factors," contained the elements that Herzberg felt truly inspired employees to perform. They included:

- Challenging work
- Opportunities for growth and advancement
- Recognition
- Impact on the organization

Table 7.1

Two dimensions of employee satisfaction.

Hygiene Factors (Dissatisfiers)	Motivators (Satisfiers)
Company policies	Work itself
Supervision	Achievement
Salary	Recognition
Interpersonal relations	Responsibility
Working conditions	Advancement

These factors, he argued, were the keys to positively motivating the work force. The most controversial part of Herzberg's model was his assertion that money fell under the hygienic, not the motivating, factors. He believed that it was the most powerful of the dissatisfiers, meaning that it is extremely dissatisfying for an employee to perceive that he or she is inadequately compensated. But Herzberg contended that money was not the positive driver of employee satisfaction, as was (and still is) popularly believed. Rather, the nature of the work itself and the perceived opportunities for growth and recognition were positioned as leading to more job satisfaction than was salary. His conclusions are consistent with the findings of studies on retention that identify the lack of challenging work and a poor relationship with their manager as the two principal reasons high-potential managers leave their companies. Compensation was a distant third.

Herzberg's model is useful in establishing a coaching agenda in working with associates. By identifying problems associates are having with the hygienic factors, you can work on minimizing their level of dissatisfaction. More importantly, coaching emphasis should be placed on the motivating factors—offering opportunities for recognition, career advancement, and professional development and providing work that is meaningfully related to the organization's strategic objectives.

One last theory of motivation that is worth noting for its relevance to managerial coaching is the equity theory proposed by Stacey Adams. This theory is derived from Adams's perspective as an organizational behaviorist. This discipline looks at how individuals relate to others within the context of an organization. Through his research, Adams determined that people are highly concerned with equity (as opposed to equality) in how they are treated by their company and their manager. If employees believe they are being treated fairly vis á vis their peers, then they are satisfied and motivated. Dissatisfaction is created where inequities exist, and this leads to a lack of motivation and reduced productivity.

Here is a simplified application of the theory: Person X evaluates the proportion of his outputs (extrinsic rewards or outcomes) over his inputs (amount of effort or level of performance) in comparison with Person Y's outputs and inputs. If Person X perceives the formula to be out of balance, he is dissatisfied with the inequity (see Figure 7.1).

Person X perceives that he is putting more into his work but getting the same rewards as Person Y. He is thus motivated to resolve the inequity. As a first step, Person X would typically seek a raise in compensation that would balance out the equation more equitably. Since pay increases are rarely granted in order to resolve these types of concerns, Person X's next step would likely be to get Person Y to improve his input. "You're not carrying your full load in this department; you need to work harder" is something X might say to Y. That tactic is rarely successful, and by now Person X is running out of options to resolve the inequity. Since it is highly unlikely that he would try to have Person Y's salary reduced, the only alternative left is for Person X to reduce his inputs in order to achieve an equitable situation—"why should I work this hard when it doesn't get me anywhere" would describe X's attitude. Person X has become demotivated due to the inequity, and it negatively impacts his job performance.

The application of equity theory for managerial coaching is focused primarily on group or team dynamics. Associates do not evaluate equitable treatment in a vacuum—they are measuring the way they are being treated in comparison with the way their peers are being treated. Therefore, you must be mindful of the perceived fairness in the way you treat your individual employees. If one of your associates perceives that you give more attention and recognition to another member of your staff, at the same time that she perceives that their job performances and effort are about the same, then she will be dissatisfied with the inequity. And it is the percep-

Figure 7.1

Equity theory of motivation.

Person X:	$\dfrac{\text{Output — 100 units}}{\text{Input — 100 units}}$
Person Y:	$\dfrac{\text{Output — 100 units}}{\text{Input — 85 units}}$

tion of the inequity that counts. It does not matter if you don't agree that there is differential treatment. If the associate perceives it, then that person's motivation is affected.

It is important to remember that you do not need to treat everybody equally but you do need to consider how you can provide your associates with outcomes that are proportionately commensurate with their levels of effort and performance. Traps to avoid include:

- Being perceived as liking some associates a lot more than others
- Spending the vast majority of your time with just a few associates
- Praising just one individual for an accomplishment when others also contributed to the success of a project
- Waiting for final results before recognizing an associate who is putting forth a good bit of effort, especially when other associates are not trying as hard

These are all examples of potentially serious inequities that could dramatically influence your unit's productivity. Coach individuals in a way that fosters perceptions of equitable treatment, and help those whose concerns of inequities are prevalent to see the situation differently when there is more equity than they perceive.

Coaching for performance is one of the three phases of developing your people. In the next chapter we will explore the manager's role as teacher to transfer knowledge and experience in order to enhance wisdom.

QUESTIONS AND EXERCISES

- Write a brief profile of a coach you admire. What are that person's key attributes? What is it about that coach that connects with you?
- Analyze your coaching behaviors as a manager. What are your strengths as a coach, and what are the areas you should work on developing?
- Consider how you could apply the three motivation models presented in this chapter to your associates. Which one(s) do you consider most relevant for your unit? How can you positively impact your associates' motivation and degree of job satisfaction over the next few months?
- In order for you to become a more effective managerial coach, you need to build coaching into your day-to-day interactions with associates. What are some of the ways in which you could start doing that immediately?

CHAPTER 8

Teaching

"Learning sleeps and snores in libraries, but wisdom is everywhere, wide awake, on tiptoes. . . ."
— Josh Billings

Over the 25 years I have worked in university administration, I have held 14 different positions and moved across 7 functional areas. My doctoral degree in adult and higher education could not be more directly associated with this type of work experience. Yet precious little of the teaching I received in the Ph.D. program prepared me to assume any of these managerial responsibilities. Virtually all my learning was accomplished through on-the-job experience and the opportunity of connecting with a few professional organizations that added a lot to my knowledge base. This is not meant as a condemnation of my graduate education but rather as illustrative of the common disconnection between academic teaching and real-world application. At the time I was taking the doctoral-level courses, I did not have enough work experience under my belt to fully appreciate the issues we were discussing. Tacit knowledge is not nearly as powerful as applied knowledge to promote real learning. My limited experience made it difficult for me to put in proper context the new information I was getting through my classes.

Fortunately, early in my career I worked for several managers who were skillful teachers of technical knowledge. I was able to quickly learn the business of foreign student advising and fundraising in the first two positions I held. The latter skill has continued to be valuable to me. I did not receive much direct instruction from my supervisors as I moved up the ladder into management positions. However, I did inherit some experienced staff members who helped me learn the important technical knowledge I needed to acquire. Luckily, the person I worked for when I first moved into executive education was a teacher by instinct. He taught me a great deal about the industry and program design. Now I am in the position of teaching others—a responsibility I take quite seriously.

The reason for this trip down memory lane is that I believe my experience is pretty typical for anyone who has moved up the managerial ranks in a complex organization. New hires are the ones most likely to be viewed as needing to be taught what to do; therefore managers focus their teaching and training efforts at that level of employee. As people move into management positions, the explicit teaching tends to disappear—yet it is no less important to the experienced manager than it is to the entry-level associate. I know that if the people I reported to when I reached director level had taught me better, it would have greatly enhanced my effectiveness and ability to step into new situations. The managerial responsibility of teaching exists at all levels of management—from the shop floor to the executive suite.

My experiences were also typical in another fashion with regard to learning on the job. The training I received from my managers was heavily focused on technical knowledge and not on leadership or strategic management issues. These are things I had to learn for myself. As a result, I have made my share of mistakes managing people and working with other departments in my organization. That is probably why I decided to focus a lot of my teaching activities on those topics—I learned their importance the hard way. And I have learned the importance of developing sound political skills, effective use of power and influence, and strategic thinking among my key staff members.

According to the dictionary, *teaching* means "to impart knowledge or skill." It is interesting to contrast that definition with the one for *training*—"to make proficient by instruction and practice." From the perspective of outcomes, training implies learning a specific task or set of activities, while *teaching* suggests broadening one's understanding or expanding one's skill set. I find this distinction useful in how I conceptualize my teaching role as a manager. Training is important, and there will always be a need to instruct people in how to accomplish specific tasks or use certain tools. For example, I have been trained in how to use a spreadsheet to develop and monitor an operating budget. But this training did not help me to better understand how to use a budget to make better management decisions. I had to be taught that skill, or, more accurately, that set of skills. Teaching requires the learner to combine new pieces of knowledge with information already gained from experience in order to achieve a higher level of learning. It is common to know how to train people, but few managers know how to effectively teach their associates. It is a critical gap in most corporations and is particularly evident in companies that are growing and lack depth in their management ranks to fill these needs internally.

This was one of the key issues at The Home Depot as it passed its twentieth year of operation. The company opened its 1,000th store in the summer of 2000, 21 years after opening the very first Home Depot in Atlanta. As it worked on executing its aggressive growth plans to reach 2,000 stores by the year 2003, the company realized it had a significant problem. Despite having thousands of assistant store managers, it did not have enough people ready to take on the job of store manager to support the rapid growth. As an organization, The Home Depot had developed a very strong training-oriented culture, but it did not sufficiently focus on teaching its associates how to prepare the next generation of managerial leaders. The difference was that its people were capable of accomplishing specific tasks associated with running a store, but they were not ready to use sound judgment in making the difficult decisions that have to be made to effectively run the business.

The best way to think about how to teach in a business context is to consider what makes for effective teaching in an educational setting. I often ask participants in our executive programs if they remember a teacher they had in school who had a strong positive influence over them. Virtually 100 percent raise their hands indicating they have had such a teacher in their past. As a follow-up question, I ask each participant to describe what made that particular teacher effective. The descriptors have been incredibly consistent across the many groups with which I have worked. The qualities and behaviors that outstanding teachers were reported to demonstrate include:

- Strong content knowledge—they know their subject well
- Passion for teaching
- Challenged students to do their best—demanding
- Built students' confidence that they could learn difficult material
- Cared for each student
- Had the ability to teach individual students in the way that best enabled the students to learn—did not use a one-size-fits-all teaching style
- Demonstrated a love for learning and helping others to learn

With one exception, this list matches well with the formula for effective teaching that I was taught in a college of education. The missing item is the mechanics of teaching—knowing how to teach a subject, from curriculum design to developing specific lesson plans. This item is implied in the descriptors from the executives, particularly with regard to the ability to adjust teaching style to meet the needs of the individual learners. That requires a fundamental knowledge of teaching techniques correlated with differing learning styles.

There is virtually no research on effective teaching in a corporate context. Therefore, the knowledge that has been learned about effective teaching from educators is important to consider. The National Commission on Teaching and America's Future (NCTAF) is the leading organization in the United States studying teaching and student learning. The Commission's vision statement, as derived from its major report, *What Matters Most: Teaching for America's Future,* is as follows: "We propose an audacious goal. . . . By the year 2006, America will provide every student with what should be his or her educational birthright: access to competent, caring and qualified teachers in schools organized for success."

I have had many interesting discussions about teaching with a close friend, Dr. Barnett Berry, who is head of policy and state partnerships for NCTAF and director of NCTAF's Southeast Center for Quality Teaching. Much of the current attention on teacher quality is focused on teacher preparation. There are significant problems with the teacher education programs run by colleges of education and with the on-the-job professional development that teachers receive once they enter the field. In less dramatic circumstances, these problems are similar in business. Managers are not adequately prepared in their educational training for the teaching roles they face, nor does anyone pay attention to developing this capability once they are on the job.

I'm not sure I have fully convinced my friend that the teaching role of managers is similar to that of professionals in our public schools. But we do agree that the essentials of teaching in any context boil down to three key abilities: expertise in the subject matter, expertise in knowing how to teach, and passion for seeing students learn.

UNDERSTANDING LEARNING

When it came to teaching college courses, a former colleague once told me that to teach well, you just had to make sure you stayed one chapter ahead of your students. I don't buy that argument. It is certainly possible to teach by keeping slightly ahead of the class, but it is not possible to teach well with that strategy. You need to have a thorough understanding of your subject matter in order to know how to help someone else learn the material. People learn by adding new information onto what they already know and then by seeing the ways in which all that information is interrelated. Teachers in any setting need to know everything about what they are teaching at the beginning in order to piece together effective learning activities.

Learning is a two-way process. In addition to having a competent teacher, there must be a receptive and motivated learner. In a business, there are clearly times when associates shut down their motivation to learn, but that is more rare than common for most people. The desire to learn exists in most of us, at least those of us who fall within McGregor's Theory Y category, even when it does not appear on the surface. The openness and motivation to learn is mostly driven by the effectiveness of the teaching.

A brief case in point: When I was just getting started in executive education, my manager encouraged me to meet with a former colleague of his—Rita—whom he considered an expert in conducting needs assessments in designing customized programs. I had just been engaged by a major company to run a custom executive program, and so this was important to me. I was highly motivated to talk with Rita about her knowledge and experience. Within five minutes of our initial meeting, Rita had managed to completely turn off my desire to listen to her. I think it was her comment, "You are so lucky to be able to learn from me," that pushed me over the edge. Rita's arrogance and level of grandiosity were way too high to suit my learning style. Granted, it was more my loss than hers, as she did have a good amount of experience that could have been useful. But due to her attitude, Rita was a totally ineffective teacher for me.

A good teacher quickly determines the student's learning style and adjusts teaching methodologies accordingly. I have not been able to find one source that provides a good description of learning styles relevant to the corporate setting. Having received a doctorate in adult education, however, I did study learning styles many years ago. Here are the important issues to keep in mind.

First and foremost, when it comes to your work as a manager, remember that you are teaching adults. They do not learn the same way children learn. Most adults have the ability to comprehend abstract concepts and to use critical thinking skills to work through a problem or situation. However, there are two important items to consider in promoting effective learning among adults:

1. The new information being taught needs to relate to something they already know.
2. They need to be able to try it themselves and apply new knowledge through direct experience in order to really learn it.

One obvious implication of these principles is to work from something familiar when trying to teach new concepts or skills to your associates. For example, taking someone from the sales force and putting that person through a rotation in the finance department is not likely to be successful unless the individual has a good finance and accounting background. The tasks are just too different. However, moving someone from manufacturing to sales, or from sales to marketing, makes more sense, as the person's past experience would typically relate better to the new functional area.

This helps to illustrate how important it is to know the complete subject matter before you begin teaching the first chapter.

As best as you can, you should determine the total set of skills and knowledge a particular associate will need to learn in preparation for the next position. With an understanding of the whole picture, you then will be able to know how to sequence the individual learning stages so they fit together coherently. As discussed in Chapter 6, one way to do this is to identify the set of specific competencies that correlate with specific positions or levels in the organization. Competency development establishes the learning agenda for associates.

Case in point: The Coca-Cola Company recently developed an extensive "competency map" that identifies the range of marketing competencies that managers should be able to demonstrate depending upon their level of marketing responsibilities. The map provides a learning blueprint, for example, for someone who wants to move from a nonmarketing job into one of the marketing functions at Coca-Cola North America. For a manager with some responsibility for teaching these competencies to his or her associates, the map creates a meaningful sequential learning agenda.

Another way to look at variations in learning styles was developed by David Kolb. He analyzed how people prefer to learn by looking at two sets of dynamics. The first dynamic distinguishes between people who would prefer to learn through active experimentation and those who would rather learn by reflective observation. Those who prefer activity want to get their hands on the new material right away. "Let me do it" would be a common expression from someone with this learning style. Reflective observation refers to individuals who like to either watch someone do something first before they try to do it themselves or to think carefully about new knowledge learned before attempting to apply it. Someone with this learning style would be likely to say, "Let me watch you do it for a while," before trying a new technique.

The second dynamic of this theory concerns the preference for learning by interacting with other people as opposed to learning individually. Some people are more comfortable learning in a group context. The energy and ideas of others helps them to put new knowledge into perspective. Someone with this style might be inclined to say, "Let's talk about this some more so I can better understand what you're telling me."

In contrast, there are individuals who prefer to learn in solitude. Interactions with others are more distracting than beneficial for them. "I would like to think about this for a while and then we can discuss it further" is the type of comment likely to come from a person who prefers to process new information alone rather than with others. This dynamic correlates closely with the extrovert-introvert scale on the Myers-Briggs Type Indicator. It has little to do with sociability but rather refers to inside-out versus outside-in thinking. Most Americans are extroverted and approach the world from an outside-to-inside orientation. They are more comfortable learning and thinking out loud with others, as opposed to reflecting on their own before discussing a topic.

Kolb put the two dynamics together and described four phases of the learning cycle presented in Figure 8.1. Each phase of the cycle represents a different learning of these preferences. An individual who prefers to learn through active experimentation combined with interacting with others has the label "accommodator." The "converger" is the person who combines active experimentation with learning individually. On the reflective observation axis, the two categories are "diverger" and "assimilator." Divergers like to learn with others, while assimilators are much more inclined to learn alone.

There is no single best style, and to some extent we use all four styles depending upon the circumstances. However, we learn best when the information is presented in the way that is most comfortable for us. People also have a tendency to pursue careers that best fit their learning style. For example, many engineers are assimilators. They prefer to digest detailed information on their own before discussing options. Many IT professionals are convergers. They prefer to work individually at first, but they also like to learn by doing, rather than by observation.

The learning style inventory is a useful tool for understanding how to adapt teaching styles to meet the needs of your associates. Get to know their individual styles and tailor your teaching activities to best fit with their preferences. For the divergers in your

Figure 8.1

Interpreting your learning style.

The model below describes the four phases of the learning cycle. There are two ways you can take in experience — by Concrete Experience or Abstract Conceptualization. There are also two ways you deal with experience — by Reflective Observation or Active Experimentation. When you use both the *concrete* and *abstract* modes to take in your experience, and when you both *reflect* and *act* on that experience, you expand your potential to completely engage in a learning process.

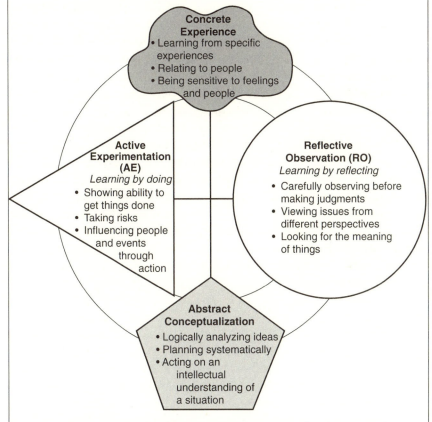

You may begin a learning process in any of the four phases of the learning cycle. Ideally, using a well-rounded learning process, you would cycle through all four phases. However, you may find that you sometimes skip a phase in the cycle or focus primarily on just one. Think about the phases you tend to skip and those you tend to concentrate on.

group, spend time discussing options as part of the learning process. Help these individuals look at a problem from several different perspectives and ask them to articulate the pros and cons of the alternatives. If you are teaching accommodators, you should focus your activities on short, succinct messages. Meet with those persons face-to-face and use your emotions and energy to reinforce the points you are making. Accommodators respond well to enthusiasm and passion in discourse. For convergers, you are more likely to reach them if you give them a brief set of directions and then let them try it for themselves. After a while, you should check their progress, offer some more suggestions on how they can refine their efforts, and then let them go at it again. Finally, with assimilators, it is important to provide them with the underlying logic of whatever you are trying to teach them. Give them a chance to process that information and then talk with them about what they have learned.

If you think you don't have the time to teach as a manager, think again. It is very possible to use daily activities as teaching opportunities. It just requires some thought and the patience to let your associates work through problems without your immediately giving them the answer. You have learned a lot in your career—pass that knowledge along to your colleagues in a way that maximizes their learning.

QUESTIONS AND EXERCISES

- Think about the one or two teachers you had in school who meant the most to you. What made those individuals effective as teachers? Make a list of those qualities and use it to help guide your teaching on the job.
- Identify the different learning styles of your key associates. What is your preferred way of learning new information? Is there a predominant style in your unit?
- Determine some routine activities that can be turned into good teaching opportunities for your staff. How can you restructure those events to optimize learning? What shifts would you expect to see in your leadership role(s)?

CHAPTER 9

Mentoring

"Wisdom is knowing what to overlook."
—Anonymous

In Homer's *Odyssey*, Mentor was the trusted adviser to Odysseus and the caring teacher of his son, Telemachus. The definition of a mentor, as applied today, is directly related to Homer's character—"a wise, loyal adviser; a teacher or coach." The integration of the three phases of development is keenly depicted in this description. The focus of this chapter will be on the advisory role of the mentor. It reflects the essence of the relationship between mentor and protégé.

Mentoring has become common as a term applied to an organizational context. Over the past decade, many companies have developed formal mentoring programs to help junior-level managers learn from wise and experienced senior-level executives. Typically, these efforts are targeted at a particular group of younger managers (high potentials, new managers, e.g.), and the structuring of the mentor program assures that each member of the target population will receive a level of advice and support from an experienced manager.

The research on the effectiveness of mentoring programs has been, at best, inconclusive, and at worst, discrediting. The variations in quality of mentoring provided and the extraneous events that impact career development make it virtually impossible to prove that structured mentoring programs work. Yet from the stories told by many of the managers with whom I have worked over the years, there is a lot of anecdotal evidence supporting the positive impact of informal mentoring activities. It is not at all uncommon to hear a successful manager talk about the valuable role that a particular mentor played in helping him or her grow both personally and professionally. The fondness that people develop for their mentors is strikingly apparent as you listen to their stories.

SEVERAL DEGREES OF DIFFICULTY

One of the major elements that impacts the mentor-protégé relationship is the degree of objectivity the mentor brings to the interactions. By not being involved in the individual's day-to-day activities, and lacking direct supervisory responsibilities, the mentor is unencumbered by some key potential conflicts that would interfere with the ability to offer sound advice. An effective mentor keeps the relationship focused solely on the needs of the protégé, not on any of his or her own personal agendas. That becomes much more difficult if the two people have a formal reporting line connection.

Thus, the mentoring component of the three phases of development can be the most challenging for the managerial leader. It is not easy to maintain a high level of objectivity in discussing career development and organizational politics with a subordinate. It is also difficult for the associate to feel secure in talking openly and honestly with her manager, as she might with a mentor who was outside the work unit. Or, as I have learned the hard way, it may not be safe to assume your manager has your best interests at heart when it comes to career development within the organization.

Case in point: In 1988, the business school dean I was working for asked me to take on a new assignment in the school to replace an administrator who had been ineffective in managing an important unit—the placement office. I had developed a modest reputation for being able to turn around troubled departments, and so this was a logical request. Since it was not a position that particularly appealed to me over the long term, I talked with the dean about what my next opportunity would be if I were able to get the placement unit back on track. He told me this would be a two-year assignment and I would be able to move into an area of the business school that was more aligned with my interests at that time. That sounded good to me, and believing the dean was sincerely interested in my career development, I agreed to the reassignment. When the two years had gone by, I discovered the dean had no intention of moving me into any other area since I had successfully alleviated a major problem for him. In his interactions with me, the dean simply said that no other alternatives were available but that I could move once an opportunity arose. I made an error in judgment by continuing to be honest with him in expressing my desire to get out of that role. My mistake was assuming the dean was a mentor instead of a manager who had his own interests at heart. This created a lot of tension between us that I did not fully understand until a few years later when I was able to look back on this experience. He wanted to minimize the problems he had to manage. If I left the placement office, the problem that had been fixed would need to be addressed again. Therefore, the dean did not want to help me find a position that was more suitable to my interests. And my constant comments about wanting to move on did nothing but irritate him. I finally learned to keep those thoughts to myself and to seek advice from others. After two more years as placement director, I was able to get the new assignment I truly desired—in executive education. This occurred because a previous mentor of mine, who happened to be a member of the faculty, used his influence to help create this opportunity.

There are times when the needs of the organization are in conflict with an individual's career aspirations—as just described in my own experience. This conflict constrains a manager from serving as a mentor to one of his or her associates. It is the exceptional person who can rise above managerial self-interests and keep the associate's needs at heart. Candor and honesty are important ingredients to help ameliorate this tension. It was disingenuous when the dean told me he would help me find a position in the business school that most fit my interests if I spent two years as the placement director. He had every right to reassign me to that job, regardless of my career aspirations. I would have operated without the pretense of thinking it was a very short-term assignment and left the discussions of my career interests out of our relationship. Once he appeared to have more of a mentoring role with me, I responded accordingly. It would have been much better to interact with him solely as my supervisor than to consider him a mentor as well.

This, coupled with other similar experiences, has taught me to be very careful in advising people who work directly for me about their careers. While I am pleased to be able to offer advice and to help them think through their potential opportunities, I consider it important to indicate that the possibilities we discuss are just that—possibilities—and should not be construed as definitive. I want those seeking advice about their careers to appreciate the potential influence that my managerial responsibilities might have on the mentoring advice I offer.

A less potentially contentious aspect of mentoring your staff members, as a managerial leader, is to help them better understand the organization's political landscape and how to best navigate it. Learning how to work the system to get things done is a very important skill set. And it is worth learning regardless of how long the associate will remain with the organization. While each company has its own set of idiosyncrasies, these skills are highly transferable. A good place to start is to encourage your associate to build a network of relationships with key individuals across the company. You can help with appropriate introductions or reasons for the contacts to be made. Often, associates rely totally on their manager's relationships with people throughout the organization in cases where their units need support and advocacy. It is in the best interests of both the manager and the associates, especially the associates, if the associates create their own networks of contacts. In this way, the associates are not entirely dependent upon the manager's reputation and sense of good standing in the company.

A related concept is to help your associates identify other mentors—especially those who might not normally pop up on the radar screen. In one of my first administrative jobs, my manager, Jay, was as new to the department as I was. In fact, I had more technical knowledge about our area, but he knew much more about the organization and the people in it. One of our colleagues, Roy, had been in the department for quite a long time and was on the verge of retirement. Five years previously, Roy had been the department head, but the job grew beyond his capacity and so he had been relegated to the role of "senior adviser." As a young, overly confident administrator, I came in challenging all the office's processes and traditions. Roy put up a good amount of resistance to any new ideas I offered. While I believe he saw some talent in me, my apparent lack of respect for the past got to him. I was becoming frustrated with his hesitance to do anything differently and complained about it to Jay. He gave me some advice that has always stuck with me. Jay helped me to appreciate Roy's circumstances and to understand why he might be resisting my suggestions. Among the pieces of information Jay passed along was the fact that Roy was epileptic and occasionally had grand mal seizures that took a lot out of him emotionally, as well as physically. Jay encouraged me to spend some time getting to know Roy personally as a way of helping us both to better appreciate the other's talents.

So I went to Roy and asked if he would be willing to talk with me about his epilepsy. (Jay had let me know Roy would be open to such a conversation or I would never have had the nerve to ask.) Most importantly, I asked Roy how I could help him should he have a seizure in the office. My naiveté made me a bit brazen, perhaps, but Roy was touched that I wanted to know. It turns out that no one else in the office had ever had this conversation with him, despite his having several seizures over the years. In fact, one of the other professionals in the office had once bear-hugged Roy while he was seizing, which served only to severely damage a few of his ribs. We also discovered a mutual interest in fishing. This was a surprise to me, as Roy was always formally dressed for the office with his shoes routinely polished. He did not seem like the outdoor type. Roy fished alone, and so he never invited me to join him. But he spent hours meticulously drawing me a map of the local lake, in which he identified all the premier fishing locations. The first time I saw him at the lake, Roy was dressed in ripped shorts, an old stained T-shirt, and no shoes. No wonder he never invited anyone to join him!

The point of this story is that Roy and I became much closer colleagues once we got past the initial defenses and barriers. Jay's advice paid off for all of us. Over the course of the next few years, prior to his retirement, Roy helped me as much as he could in understanding the past so I could help shape the future. We continued to have our disagreements about how fast things should change, but we had a healthy respect for each other that enabled us to make progress.

KEYS TO EFFECTIVE MENTORING

Remember, the point of mentoring is to provide advice and guidance on career and other long-term development issues. When I have asked managers to describe the attributes of a good mentor, these are the descriptors most often cited:

- Good listener
- Has my best interests at heart
- Has a lot of wisdom from personal experiences
- Trustworthy and candid
- Understands the politics in the organization
- Seems to enjoy watching others succeed

Recognizing that they were describing traditional senior-level executives as mentors, note that the list fits managers just as well. If you exemplify these characteristics, you will be able to serve a mentoring role with your staff.

Here are some ways in which you can integrate mentoring into your activities:

- Meet with your associates once or twice a year to discuss their career progress and aspirations; take notes so you can recall the conversations and see how their plans change over time.
- Get to know your associates' family situations and principal hobbies or community activities; this helps round out your perspective on who they are and what's important to them.
- If one of your associates is struggling with a career or professional decision, let the associate know you would be willing to offer your advice; try to avoid giving advice without being invited to do so.
- Demonstrate empathy for the situations your associates are facing, perhaps by recalling similar experiences you had to address.
- Use storytelling from your past to describe how you learned to manage your own career, especially relating to mentors who provided guidance to you.
- Encourage your associates to continue to grow and develop meaningful careers for themselves, even if that means leaving your unit to pursue other opportunities.

I have been fortunate over the span of my managerial career to have worked with many outstanding associates. A number of the relationships that were developed continued well after the point we stopped working together. It gives me enormous personal satisfaction to know I have helped others grow personally and professionally. Mentoring can be the most rewarding of the three developmental activities.

QUESTIONS AND EXERCISES

- Try to identify individuals within your organization who are considered to be good mentors to people at your level. What are their personal characteristics that enable them to be good mentors?
- Who has been a mentor to you? How did that person help you?
- What mentoring experiences have you had in helping others? What were the circumstances, and how were you able to assist them?
- From the perspective of mentoring, which of your personal characteristics are most suited to this role? Which are least suited to mentoring?
- For each of your key staff members, can you identify their career objectives over the next five years? Are you aware of any major decisions they are currently facing, or likely to face in the next few months? How could you help them as a mentor?

CHAPTER 10

Developing Self and Developing Others

"Now's the day, and now's the hour."

—Robert Burns

Unlearning is harder than learning, especially for adults. The behaviors people exhibit are typically built from the experiences they have had over many years. It is quite a challenge, first, to understand what we need to change in ourselves and, second, to do something about it that makes a difference. Before you begin to work on helping your associates change their leadership practices, you need to work on your own behaviors. There is no substitute for "walking the talk" as a source of modeling and inspiration.

Case in point: Stuart was the founder and president of a marketing services firm. His background was primarily in working behind the scenes in major political campaigns. Stuart was skillful, and his reputation spread to the point where he was asked to consult for some businesses and major not-for-profit organizations. Stuart's very small company of 3 people grew over a few years to become a moderately sized marketing firm of 25+ employees. As with many entrepreneurs whose talents are well suited to creating a business, as opposed to maintaining one, Stuart began to realize he was working too hard doing tasks he had hired others to perform. His excitement was in developing new business and in serving as a strategic adviser to the key accounts. Stuart was not able to spend significant amounts of time in either of those areas because he was constantly putting out fires, reviewing and revising marketing campaigns his staff created for clients, and dealing with personnel problems. For a variety of reasons, the people he had hired to handle the more routine tasks were not reducing his need to spend time on these issues. As the business grew, Stuart was becoming more and more disenchanted with his work life. After a few heart-to-heart talks with some of his key associates, and with himself, Stuart realized the problems might be more with him than with his staff. His people were not developing their skills beyond the technical talents they brought with them into the company. It took a couple of years before Stuart began to consider how he might be contributing to that reality.

The staff had learned that Stuart would review their creative work and change it to suit his style before sending it to the clients. Therefore, they anticipated his micromanagement of their work and loaded Stuart up with materials to approve. There were no negative consequences for doing work he did not accept. And Stuart was not highly skilled at interpersonal communications in areas involving emotions, and so he did not offer constructive criticism to anyone. Because he was not disseminating the wisdom he had gained over the years, the staff were not learning how to improve their skills to meet his quality demands. Stuart did not coach his staff to perform at a higher level since he viewed his role as primarily in client services rather than as a developer of his staff. The result was that Stuart performed his staff's duties rather than his duties as leader of the organization. Neither did he talk with his key associates about how they could better develop their capabilities in order to grow within the business and the industry as a whole. Morale was low. The company was constantly behind in meeting client deadlines. Some of Stuart's best people left the firm to pursue other opportunities, and he was having a difficult time finding good replacements. Most importantly, Stuart was seriously considering selling the company and trying something else. He was very unhappy with the way things had developed and missed the fun he had when he was building the business.

It was at this point that Stuart began to look at his own leadership practices to see if he could find some answers. What he discovered, with some help from external coaches, was that he was not adequately developing his people. There was no coaching, teaching, or mentoring. Stuart tried a different approach and met with the whole staff to discuss some of his beliefs in how to best serve clients. His passion for the work was obvious, and his associates were very responsive to his lessons. They wanted more and were able to effectively communicate that to Stuart. As he spent more time passing along his knowledge, their work began to improve. Some of the more talented associates on the creative side of the agency came up with new concepts that used Stuart's teaching as a foundation but that took his ideas to a higher level. Progress was slow and, at times, inconsistent, but the momentum had begun to shift. As Stuart was able to spend less time doing the work himself due to the enhanced quality of the work done by his associates, his attitude improved. This directly improved morale within the agency, which fed back into making Stuart more satisfied with his work.

CREATING AN ENVIRONMENT THAT ENCOURAGES PERSONAL DEVELOPMENT

The important concept to recognize is that you cannot separate developing others from developing yourself. Good coaches know they get better as a result of coaching their players. Good teachers realize they learn as much from their students as their students learn from them. Discussing how to work through the political environment within the organization with a protégé helps the mentor achieve more clarity about how to do that successfully. By putting your attention into coaching, teaching, and mentoring others, you will also be developing yourself. If you are truly open to understanding your emotions and to learning new behaviors, you will become a better managerial leader.

The more you model effective leadership practices, the more your associates will follow your example and enhance their leadership skills as well. Evidence supporting this argument abounds. You have undoubtedly seen it for yourself. If you find a unit that is performing well, with motivated employees who work well together, the probability is high that a primary reason for their success is that the unit's manager is an effective leader. In contrast, it would be expected that a poorly performing unit that is suffering from low morale, and in which there is a distinct lack of cooperation among the associates, has a manager who does not know how to lead in today's world. When you enhance your leadership practices, you raise everyone around you to a higher level of achievement. Therefore, if you are prepared to work hard at becoming more of a developmental manager, look to create an environment that is development-focused for everyone within your span of control in the organization, including yourself. Here are 10 steps you can take to help you create that kind of environment:

1. Go public with your intent to focus on development. Let it be known that each associate has the ultimate responsibility for his or her own development. Your responsibility is to enable their development by providing resources, opportunities, and support.
2. Using a retreat format, have an open discussion with your staff to assess your unit's current strengths and deficiencies. Be candid in this assessment—starting with an honest dialog about your own capabilities and shortcomings. Use the deficiencies that were identified to determine the competencies that are the most important to your unit's future success. This should help you create a blueprint for development on an organizational scale upon which you can base individual development plans.
3. Demonstrate what this means by using yourself as an example. From this blueprint, look for an opportunity that will help you grow professionally and allocate the time to gain this experience. It would be particularly meaningful if the activity you selected were focused on improving your skills at developing others. Let your associates know what skills and competencies you want to develop.
4. Have each of your associates create a development plan that is aligned with the competency gaps that were identified. Review the plans with each person to offer your perspectives on the areas they should work on first. Help them identify opportunities to build the identified skills and come up with a timetable to which you will hold them accountable.
5. Conduct some type of 360° feedback on your leadership behaviors. Find a meaningful mechanism that would provide you with candid feedback from your associates specifically on your leadership practices (as opposed to your business and management skills). This should be done at

the beginning stages of your efforts to provide you with the "pretest" data. After six to nine months, you should conduct a second round of feedback as a "posttest" to measure your progress.

6. Build the elements of coaching, teaching, and mentoring into your regular activities. Specifically with regard to their development plans, your coaching should be concentrated on motivating the associates to keep working toward their objectives and on helping them adjust their plans as they go. Make sure you are teaching them skills that fit the development plan. And as their mentor, help them envision the long-term rewards of their professional growth as they make progress.

7. Plan and organize a developmental activity that would involve the entire staff. This should be tied to the competency list that was generated (see step 2). For example, if one of the deficiencies in your unit is efficiency in managing projects, then you could hire someone to teach a one-day class on project management tools.

8. Encourage your associates to become involved in community activities that would help them grow, both personally and professionally. Serving on boards of not-for-profit organizations, being a coach of a recreational sports team for children, and tutoring kids at a local school are all illustrations of civic-minded volunteer activities that develop professional competencies.

9. Find meaningful ways to encourage, reward, and recognize progress made by your associates as they enhance their capabilities. Currently, I have a member of my staff who has decided to take evening classes in order to complete her undergraduate degree. She has about two years' worth of courses to take, and every one of her colleagues and I are supporting her efforts. We will make sure she is able to leave work early in order to get to her classes. We will also help her as needed with studying and will celebrate each time she completes one of her course requirements all the way through graduation. Her accomplishment will become

our accomplishment to the extent that we all want her to achieve this goal.

10. Continue to remind your associates that they need to seek developmental opportunities. If you have the resources available, you could allocate a certain amount of money to each staff member to use only on a self-development activity. You may choose to broadly define the range of activities that could be included—from business seminars to wellness center fees. The only payback you should require is some report back to the rest of the staff of what people-learned or how that activity helped them. This builds a sense of mutual accountability.

Case in point: The Lend Lease Corporation is a real estate investment company based in Australia. The company has grown considerably in the United States, primarily via acquisitions. The Australian leadership of the firm created an internal organization known as "Foundation." They reinvested capital into this entity for a number of years until it had a substantial funding base—in the millions of dollars. The company created a board of directors for the Lend Lease Foundation that was composed of employees from multiple levels across the firm. The use of the funds each year was determined by the board—the senior executives had little influence over the decisions. The only caveat was that the funds had to be used for the benefit of the employees in ways other than monetary rewards. These funds were used for tuition reimbursement, child-care subsidies, training programs, wellness activities, and celebrations. One of the most appreciated Foundation expenditures was the annual allocation of several hundred dollars for each employee to spend as he or she wished—on a self-development activity. The downside of this generosity in supporting employees was the business reality of funds not always being available. In 2000, Lend Lease sold off a major portion of the Australian part of the company, which resulted in a significant drop in the company's profitability. As a result, there weren't sufficient funds in Foundation to continue the personal allocations. Morale across the company took a hit when it was announced these would be discontinued in 2001.

There's an important message in this anecdote. Once you start down the path of encouraging and supporting development activities, associates will actively respond. It is difficult to go backward and cut these types of activities once your associates have begun to appreciate them. It is not necessarily a sense of entitlement that ensues, but more a hunger that is being fed by your support of their development. Once you start feeding the hunger, it will continue to grow. It is best to begin with small steps and work your way up than to start with a large effort and wind up having to work your way down.

The more you are able to have your associates accept the responsibility for their own development, the less likely their activities will be as susceptible to business conditions as the foundation was at Lend Lease.

QUESTIONS AND EXERCISES

- Contact your human resource manager to determine if any leadership effectiveness assessment tools are available to you through the company. If no one in the company has any experience with 360° feedback instruments, you can contact the local chapters of the Human Resource Planning Society (HRPS), American Society for Training and Development (ASTD), or the Society for Human Resource Management (SHRM) for referrals.

- Even if you have to create your own, have your associates complete a feedback survey that will provide you with their assessments of your leadership practices. Your questions should be focused on just a few key areas you have identified as priorities for enhancing your leadership skills.

- Meet with each of your associates to provide your perspective on the developmental areas on which they should concentrate this year. Help them to create a development plan to address those needs.

PART THREE

MANAGERIAL LEADERSHIP IN ACTION

CHAPTER 11

Giving and Receiving Feedback

"Feedback is the breakfast of champions."
—Ken Blanchard

One of my favorite case studies on leadership is the 1984 Harvard Business School publication "Peter Browning and Continental White Cap." This is a classic in the field of leading change and organizational transformation. It is rare to use a case study that is more than five years old in an executive program, as the material becomes quickly dated. But the Browning case is timeless. It continues to resonate with managers and executives in customized executive programs as if it were their company that was being presented.

The main character, Peter Browning, has become well known as an effective leader of corporate change. He is currently the CEO of Sonoco Products Corporation, a global packaging company headquartered in South Carolina. I became acquainted with Browning because Sonoco Products was an executive education client at the University of South Carolina. We had the opportunity to talk in depth about leadership and organizational change. His first rule of leading change was "communicate, communicate, communicate." Browning walks the talk (or, more appropriately, talks the talk), as he is an excellent communicator who finds a way to speak directly without being sharply critical.

In the Continental White Cap case, Browning has inherited a human resources manager, Mr. Green, who is barely competent. In his initial one-on-ones with his management team, Browning gave some pretty tough feedback to Green. He told him that "none of your peers around the company think that you are a strong HR manager" and "none of the staff wants to work with you." Rather than stopping there, Browning went on to say, "and you will never get a chance to succeed in this job unless you know this and get a chance to respond." He told Green to go find out for himself by talking with his staff and fellow HR managers at other Continental divisions. After doing so, Green reported, "You're right; and the thing that is really alarming is that nobody's ever told me this before."

In the previous chapter, I suggested you meet with each of your associates to review their development plans. It is critically important in this process that you provide them with open and candid feedback if you are sincerely interested in helping them to become more successful. Most managers have a very hard time giving constructive criticism. The problem seems to be more with the constructive part than with the criticism. If you want to help someone develop, you need to point out their shortcomings while providing them with a mechanism for improvement. Browning's comments to his HR manager demonstrate this balance. He could have bluntly said, "Everyone believes you're incompetent" and left it at that. That would have been candid, but also destructive. By inviting Green to go out and learn more about how he was perceived by others, Browning was offering Green the chance to turn those perceptions around by enhancing his performance—a great illustration of constructive criticism in action.

Of course, this is easier said than done. The act of giving negative feedback taps into a manager's emotions. If he or she is not comfortable using emotions to manage others, then the task can be quite threatening. Most people avoid these types of situations— they simply fail to give candid, negative feedback when it is warranted. Others have trouble controlling their emotional responses, and so they overcompensate by being either overly critical or overly consolatory. This is one of my developmental areas, as I would much prefer to be encouraging and positive with a staff member than critical and negative. However, if associates are not aware of their shortcomings, they cannot possibly work on overcoming them.

I tried the Browning approach when I first arrived at USC's Daniel Management Center. One of the four managers in the department (I'll call her Carla) was identified by every one on the staff as the primary source of discord and noncooperation in the Center. In my initial face-to-face meeting with Carla, I addressed this topic and told her that teamwork was a high priority for me. Therefore, I expected Carla to improve how she worked with the other staff members. Following the Browning strategy, I invited Carla to talk with her colleagues to find out for herself how they perceived the difficulties she created in the Center's work environment. Right strategy, wrong person. Carla never made the rounds since she was not at all interested in changing her behaviors. Constructive feedback won't work with someone who is not in any way introspective and open to self-improvement.

John, my predecessor as director, unfortunately had consistently rated Carla as "meeting" or "exceeding" expectations in all 12 of her annual performance reviews. John did so despite the fact that he had threatened to fire Carla many times for her inability to work with her colleagues and her insubordinate attitude. I tried hard but unsuccessfully to help Carla improve her teamwork and service performance to customers over an 18-month period. Eventually, I was forced to terminate her appointment at the Center, which was no minor event given that it was a state governmental agency and Carla had received nothing but satisfactory evaluations until I arrived. Because of the lack of constructive feedback that was given to her over the years, the behaviors that were dysfunctional to the organization were reinforced rather than eliminated.

It is important to the entire organization that you overcome the discomfort and provide candid feedback to your associates. The communication skills required for doing so may seem basic but are really quite refined. In providing constructive feedback you are truly helping associates have the opportunity to perform at a high level. It is good for their development. It is good for the organization's performance. It is also good for your development and leadership effectiveness.

Here are some of the principal elements for giving comprehensive feedback to an associate, especially if the feedback is in the form of constructive criticism. It is a similar framework for conducting a performance appraisal process, but the assumption is that this feedback is more focused and timely.

1. Find a location to meet that is nonthreatening and conducive to an informal discussion rather than one that
   might create a feeling of a formal hearing.
2. State the purpose of the meeting, the process of how the
   conversation will flow, and the payoff or outcome you are
   anticipating.
3. Begin by stressing the positive. Talk about things the associate is doing well or ways in which he or she is positively contributing to the unit's successes.
4. When you are getting into the areas of poor performance,
   be sure to separate the person from the problem. Do not
   make the criticism personal, but rather focus attention on
   the issues or difficulties that are created by the associate's
   actions.
5. Ask the associate to provide his or her perspective on the
   situation. Give the person the opportunity to explain or
   clarify but try to avoid having him or her become defensive or accusatory of others.
6. Be sure to listen well. You may learn something about the
   situation you did not know. You will also promote candid
   communications by demonstrating that you are willing to
   listen attentively to the person's opinions.
7. Summarize what you have heard and then offer your perspective on the matter. Remember to use "I" messages in
   personalizing the emotions—"I cannot do my job effectively when there is this level of dissent among the
   staff"—rather than putting the emotions on the associate,
   as in "You are creating a very high level of distress within
   the organization."
8. Specifically address the behavior or competency area that
   you want to see improved. Make sure both of you are
   clear on what needs to be done.
9. Set tangible milestones or accomplishments that would
   demonstrate the associate's successful improvement.
10. Create a mutually agreed-upon action plan that has a
    clear time line and date that you will meet again to
    review the progress made. End the conversation on a

positive, not punitive, note. If you are serious in your desire to see improvement, you need to show confidence that the individual can, in fact, make that improvement.

These steps are effective in most circumstances where a corrective action must be taken or where a significant performance deficiency needs to be improved. There are certainly other times when constructive feedback does not require this level of depth.

Ken Blanchard and Spencer Johnson advocated giving very short bits of feedback to associates in their book, *The One Minute Manager*. I consider constructive feedback to be more than simple forms of praise, such as "Good job" or "Thank you for your good work today." Those expressions are important and are used all too infrequently in companies today. But feedback has a different purpose than quick recognition. It is a communications activity that provides a meaningful reaction to something—a way of expressing a perception that is intended to be useful to the receiver for continuing or revising an action.

This was the type of developmental communication that Stuart's associates were thirsty for in his marketing agency. As he wandered around the office, Stuart began to stop by and talk with the creative designers while they were working on projects. Stuart would provide quick and constructive feedback such as; I like your use of color in this ad, but we need to make sure the client's product is the item that receives the attention—not the artistic design. Why don't you try placing the product here? From my perspective, that will both highlight the product and maintain the wonderful design. What do you think?

This type of feedback made quite a difference to the staff. It was an effective way for Stuart to teach his way of approaching design. Notice that in his comments, Stuart:

- Started with a positive comment
- Focused on the problem, not the person
- Offered an alternative way of handling the task and explained why he thought it was effective
- Asked for a reaction in a nonthreatening manner

Virtually every day there are opportunities for these types of exchange with your staff members. To take advantage of the opportunities, you first need to be interacting with your associates in their work space. Then you have to view your interactions from a developmental perspective—how can you help your associates learn something or build their skills today? Finally, you need to be able to communicate your feedback in a way that will enable the other person to listen without feeling overly criticized.

IT'S A TWO-WAY STREET

How feedback is received is as important as how it is given. There is another set of skills associated with effectively receiving feedback. Industrial psychologists and organizational development specialists will all tell you that "receiving feedback is a gift; you should cherish it." Sometimes it sure doesn't feel like much of a gift; and since you don't get a receipt, it's hard to take it back to the store and exchange it for something else. But you do need to find out how others perceive your behaviors or if you are doing anything incorrectly without realizing it. In that sense, receiving feedback is indeed a gift. You cannot address a problem if you are not aware of its existence.

In an ideal communications world, this would not be an issue, as individuals within the organization would be giving and receiving feedback constantly. However, there is no ideal communications world of which I am aware. Most corporate cultures reflect a lack of candor and openness in interpersonal interactions. Poor internal communications is among the most common problems identified in employee surveys addressing morale and job satisfaction. Therefore, since it is so uncommon, when people begin to receive constructive feedback, it can be very powerful. This is why organizations need to be careful when instituting 360° feedback initiatives. The first few times managers receive this intense burst of feedback it can be overwhelming. As a buffer, companies need to provide individual coaching sessions to help managers put the 360° feedback into perspective and generate an action plan as well.

Learning how to receive feedback is a skill I continue to address. As your confidence grows, you do not need to rely as heavily on your defense mechanisms to protect your ego. Earlier in my career, I was more defensive than I am now due to the insecure feelings I had about my capabilities. I can look back now and remember instances when someone was trying to give me feedback that I just could not accept at the time. Fortunately, I have improved my receptivity to constructive criticism as I have matured. Now, it is much more likely I would seek out feedback to improve my performance than to build barriers so as to avoid receiving any bad news.

In the past 17 years, I have received only one annual performance review. And the one I received (from an accounting professor) was conducted poorly! Because of this lack of formalized feedback, I have sought alternative ways of getting information about people's perceptions of my performance. At times, I have asked an experienced colleague to conduct confidential interviews of my staff regarding my leadership effectiveness in order to get constructive feedback. Certainly, I am not alone in proactively seeking feedback when the corporate culture does not naturally provide it. For years, Jim Reese, CEO of North America for Randstad Corporation, has regularly solicited written feedback from his associates on his leadership performance. Jim sees this as a double win. The information has helped him identify behaviors to change, and the activity demonstrates to Jim's staff that their perceptions about his capabilities are important to him.

As with giving feedback, there are ways to enhance your ability to receive feedback effectively as well. Remind yourself to:

- Avoid getting defensive, even if comments are expressed with a sharp edge to them.
- Listen carefully; if you start thinking about your defense while you are feeling attacked, you cannot pay attention well to what is being said; wait until you hear all the feedback before you attempt to respond.
- Ask questions for clarification, if needed, but avoid asking questions that would attack the credibility of the source.

- Thank the sender for giving you the feedback (even if you don't like what was said).

The way in which you receive feedback today will have a significant influence over the frequency and type of feedback you get tomorrow. This is especially true for subordinates. They will learn quickly how open you are to constructive criticism. If you want to hear their opinions and perceptions, then you need to create an atmosphere in the office that is conducive to their giving you feedback.

If you receive criticism for behaviors that you either cannot change or do not wish to change, then you should honestly respond to the individuals who provided the feedback. You should still listen carefully to their comments and thank them for speaking up. Then, present your reasons for not addressing their concerns at this time. Those individuals do not have to agree with you, but they should respect the choices you make if you can communicate a reasonable response.

Bob Staton, the CEO of Colonial Life & Accident Insurance Company, understood this point well. He participated in the leadership development program that was designed for the company, as did all the other managers in the company. Bob's 360° feedback was pretty rugged. He took it well and openly shared the data with anyone who was interested. Most importantly, Bob solicited help from his management team to hold him accountable to the leadership behaviors he identified in his action plan as needing to change. As he told the managers, "I may bark at first when you tell me that I am acting in a way that is contrary to my action plan, but I will listen to you and thank you later for helping me. I want you to give me this feedback."

If you do nothing else but work on your interpersonal communications skills over the next few years, you will improve your leadership effectiveness. It is the most important core competency for effective coaching, teaching, and mentoring.

QUESTIONS AND EXERCISES

- How well do you listen? How could you improve your listening skills? You spend at least 75 percent of your time listening when you communicate with others. It is a very important skill to develop.
- What was the most effective performance review you experienced? What were the qualities that made it so effective?
- How often do you walk around the office and stop into people's offices to solicit their opinions about what's going on with the unit? What could you learn that could be helpful to you?
- When was the last time you were strongly criticized by your supervisor? What did it feel like to you? How could that interaction have been handled differently to make it more effective with regard to your development?

CHAPTER 12

Managing Up and Across

"Good, the more Communicated, more abundant grows."

— John Milton, *Paradise Lost*

Managerial leadership is inherently multidimensional. As a manager in the middle of an organization, in addition to the obvious leadership challenges associated with managing others, there are also challenges of interacting with the executives above and peers across the company. To be effective, a managerial leader needs to "manage up" and to develop a network of relationships throughout the enterprise to get things accomplished.

Organizations have become increasingly complex due to the influences of globalization and the need to respond fast to market dynamics. Companies have disbanded traditional functional organizational structures in favor of more sophisticated designs of strategic business units that are built around customer segments or major product lines. The resulting multifaceted organizational structures go beyond a simple 2 x 2 matrix design with chains of command and reporting relationships that are much less clear than in a functional organization. This places a premium on an individual's ability to develop meaningful relationships that cut across divisional and functional lines.

The Fluor Daniel Corporation provides a case in point. In the mid-1990s, the company replaced a functional organizational structure with one designed around business units in major customer segments, such as paper, mining, automotive, and chemicals. The functional specialties were then deployed across the SBUs, including engineers and project managers. A third organizational dimension concerned geographic location. This dimension had two components—the physical location of the home offices and the geographic location of the individual construction projects.

The Americas Group, for example, consisted of managers and field representatives who had expertise in working in the Latin American region. If the automotive SBU were working on building a plant in Brazil, the Americas unit would provide in-country support to assist the project team in understanding the specific dynamics of operating in Brazil.

Therefore, an aspiring project manager with Fluor Daniel operates in a highly complex system. He has no single manager responsible for his performance and development. There is an existing functional hierarchy for project managers, but due to its small size it cannot provide consistent support to the associates. The individual will wind up reporting through the particular SBU to which he is assigned, but that can change as he works on projects that span across different units. Then, there is some reporting relationship to the regional or field office that serves the project location.

At the company's request several years ago, I conducted a seminar on "effective delegation" for project managers. One of the principles of delegation is its importance in developing people. Giving people more and more responsibility prepares them for moving to the next level in the organization. This became a topic of considerable discussion among the project managers in the program. Their predominant attitude was that delegating more tasks to junior-level people was not beneficial to the project manager. It slowed down their progress on a specific project, as these individuals were not prepared to function at as high a level as the experienced managers. Yes, it accelerated the development of the associates, but there was no direct benefit to the project manager—the payoff was going to come to the project managers who worked with that associate in the future. Since a project manager may never work with a particular associate again, the project manager had no vested interest in that associate's long-term development. In the complexity of this matrix, no one has daily responsibility over the growth and development of the technical managers inside the organization. Thus, the ability of associates to manage their own development and to establish a network of relationships to further their growth in the company is extremely important.

MANAGING UP

In the past 15 years, I have reported to 12 different managers. The range of personalities, leadership styles, and managerial effectiveness among this group covers a wide spectrum. Fortunately, I can honestly say I have never worked for a really poor manager—certainly, never for someone who was a severe micromanager or extraordinarily narcissistic. I have a different working relationship from other faculty members in that I have direct administrative responsibilities as opposed to having a tenure-track academic research position. In this regard, my reporting relationship to my manager is more similar to what you would find in a corporate environment than an academic one. This is especially relevant in the area of executive education, a profit center, which places me in the position of having to meet specific financial objectives.

Of the 12 managers I have reported to, 3 were from corporate backgrounds (including a former vice chairman of IBM) and the rest were professors who had moved into university administration. Each one taught me something with respect to managerial leadership, and having this variety of supervisors has helped me to appreciate the importance of building a solid working relationship from the start.

The number of managers I encounter who tell tales of difficult relationships with their bosses continues to startle me. For some the problem is one of neglect or disinterest—their boss is located in another city or region and they rarely have contact except to review business results. For others, the difficulties lie more in strong personality conflicts and inflexibility in accepting new ways of approaching the business. This is of particular concern to high-potential managers who want to see their company be more innovative only to be thwarted by a layer of overly conservative upper middle managers who are doing everything possible to avoid being replaced by the same high potentials. Research by organizations such as The Conference Board has documented that one of the main reasons talented managers leave their firms is having problems with their immediate supervisor. You cannot solely rely on luck that you will be working for an effective manager. You can, and must, contribute to your manager's effectiveness by learning how to "manage up." Consider your situation with the people who report to you. Does their behavior influence how you manage them? It would be surprising if that were not the case. Some of your associates know how to help you manage them better. They read your cues and know how to remind you to act when they realize you need to be reminded. By helping you do your job, these associates are also helping themselves through the respect and appreciation that is generated.

Expressing the importance of establishing a positive working relationship with your manager is not overstating the obvious. There may be circumstances that cannot be altered, to the point where it may be impossible to build such a relationship. But you must try hard to avoid this difficulty—for it is a significant one. Here are some of the tips I have learned from others as well as from my own experiences:

1. *Gain congruence over what you are to accomplish.* Be sure you have some agreement over the goals for your unit and how they fit into the larger organizational perspective. It seems simple, but it isn't. Financial objectives or other quantitative measures may be tangible but still may lack clarity. And there are always intangible expectations that you will be held accountable for—make sure you identify them as early as possible and discuss how they will be evaluated. The best way to get these out in the open is to ask, "What else do you want me to be sure to accomplish?" If you cannot be that direct with your manager, then be alert to significant cues. Try to determine what intangible factors your manager is most concerned about; such factors might include, for example, relationships with key executives, a good reputation for project management, or a department that is respected for its fiscal management.

2. *Communicate, communicate, communicate.* If you fail to keep your manager informed of your progress (or lack thereof) and any problems you are experiencing, then you will be at the mercy of other more filtered sources. Especially in high-visibility activities, or in highly internally competitive organizations, you can be certain that the grapevine will be working against you. Be proactive. Rather than waiting for

your manager to ask you for information when he (or she) wants it, ask how you can best keep him (or her) up to date on your activities. Try to establish a communications schedule with your manager from the beginning—for example, weekly email updates or biweekly face-to-face meetings.

3. *Tailor your communication to suit your manager's style.* Remember the learning style inventory discussed in Chapter 8. There are differences in the way people prefer to receive information. If your manager has a style similar to an accommodator (which is the most common learning style among senior managers), then your written communications should be succinct, kept to one page, with bullet points and short summaries. If, however, your manager has more of the assimilator style, then your updates should be more in the form of written reports with a reasonable level of detailed analysis. Consistent with communications theory, be sure you adapt your communication to satisfy your audience's preferences, not your own.

4. *Learn how your manager is being managed.* Help your boss to look good to his or her boss. In order to do so, you must first determine the performance measures that are used to evaluate your manager's effectiveness. The best way to figure this out is simply to ask. You may not get the whole story, but you will probably learn enough to see how you can contribute to your manager's success.

5. *Solicit informal feedback.* Don't wait for the annual performance review meeting to get your small dose of feedback. Check with your manager periodically to ask if you are performing at the appropriate levels and if he or she has any recommendations for improvement. If nothing else, this will help prevent your being surprised at the annual review meeting.

6. *Be sure to bring bad news to the boss.* Do not try to hide poor results or wait to have to explain why things were not going well when asked. Your manager cannot help solve problems about which he or she is unaware. Openness and candor about the business are very important.

7. *Bring a solution.* However, when you bring bad news to the boss, come prepared to make a recommendation for solving the problem. You want to avoid being perceived as whining or incapable of dealing with issues. Some problems have levels of complexity that require advice or support from your superior(s). Therefore, your recommendation may be incomplete, but bring the best analysis possible to the discussion.

8. *Do not speak ill of your colleagues.* Avoid criticizing others inside the organization for problems that arise. Focus on the problem, not the personalities. If your manager asks for your opinion about one of your colleague's capabilities, give a credible response but be diplomatic.

9. *Be positive.* Keep your attitude upbeat and optimistic. If you are more of the pessimist, take care not to come across as overly negative. If you are naturally optimistic, take advantage of your positive perspective but avoid coming across as too much the Pollyanna. Keep in mind what you want from your subordinates—a "can-do" attitude that is based in reality.

10. *Be careful.* I have learned the hard way that you should not believe (without significant proof) that your manager only has your best interests at heart. If you have developed a decent working relationship, you may feel you can be very candid about your career aspirations and feelings about your current position. Remember that the probabilities are greater that your manager is more interested in what is good for the company than what is good for you. Your candor could create a concern that you are looking to move elsewhere or that your motivation is not at the highest level. That will not help you.

11. *Maintain your perspective.* Situations are rarely as bad, or as good, as they appear. If you are in a difficult relationship with your manager, consider the lessons you are learning from the experience. Continue to build your internal network and avoid speaking derogatorily of your manager in public. If you are in a very positive working relationship

with your boss, enjoy the benefits but do not begin to feel invincible. And be mindful of the potential complications from jealous peers who may regard you as the "teacher's pet."

Many people do not take seriously the need to "manage up"; or at least they do not believe they can have any significant influence over their relationship with their boss. I believe this is short-sighted. Certainly, personality plays a major role in establishing the dynamic between subordinate and manager. But effort put forward to enhance that rapport can be very effective. In this regard, at least, I believe you make your own luck. This relationship is too important for you to rely on circumstance or good fortune.

MANAGING ACROSS

Of all the managerial directions, the horizontal (or perhaps diagonal) linkages are the ones that are most often ignored. You have to attend to managing your people (down), and at some point you learn that you should try to manage the relationship with your boss (up). So, with everything you must attend to, why should you worry about your relationships across the enterprise at the peer or colleague level? Answer: Because, increasingly, you have to build your internal network in order to be effective in performing your responsibilities. And it is in the best interest of your organization that these relationships and informal communication pathways get developed.

Imagine you are a district manager in a financial services company. The firm is organized to serve customers geographically, but due to increasing industry consolidation among one of your major customer segments, there are times when one client operates in several of your geographic regions. Your district is the home for this client, and so you have the principal accountability—and the profitability for this client shows up on your profit and loss statement. The other district managers do not have any incentive to service your client since it provides them with very little financial benefit for the time required in offering the service. Therefore, their service level to your customer is mediocre to poor. The lack of service consistency is beginning to impact your relationship with the client, because your client doesn't see the distinction between one geographic location to another. The client expects excellent service regardless of location. How can you improve this situation?

One answer is to change the accounting system so that the profitability is more distributed to provide the appropriate incentives for the other districts. That is obviously something you are unlikely to make happen—at least, not in the short term. Another answer is to completely restructure the service organization around customers instead of using geography. Good luck, again. The third option is for you, as district manager, to contact your peers in the other key locations and to seek their help in assuring your client gets excellent service. Perhaps your response is "Good luck, again!" However, it is the most pragmatic of the alternatives and should not be that difficult. But to make it work there has to be an established network of relationships among the district managers already in place. They create a parallel organizational structure, operating as a virtual unit that is aligned along customer segments when that is required and disappearing back to the regional model when it is no longer required.

The personal and organizational benefits of having this horizontal network in place for midlevel managers are not always visible. Take the case of Burlington Industries that was briefly described in Chapter 6. The company was left with eight divisions after its LBO in the 1980s. Each division operated virtually as an independent company with few horizontal linkages. The individual divisions did not even realize how much they overlapped with regard to customers and competitor information. It wasn't until the Leadership Development Program in 1993, conducted at the University of North Carolina for the high-potential managers across the eight divisions, that a network began to be created across the company. Once the managers identified the learning opportunities from sharing knowledge, they realized the importance of these cross-divisional horizontal relationships. Until that time, there was no visible critical issue that could have forced the managerial network to form. It works better when it happens informally at first, as trust levels are created through personal interactions that are not necessarily focused on critical business concerns.

Customized executive education programs can serve as an excellent vehicle for boosting the power of the horizontal network among key managers. Strong relationships are formed when (approximately) 40 people from across a company come together for an intensive, highly interactive learning experience of reasonable length (at least 10 days). If repeated often enough, this can create a strong web of horizontal relationships across business units in a global enterprise.

The Lockheed Martin Corporation understands this important benefit. In the Strategic Leadership Development Program (SLDP) that Emory University conducts for director-level managers across the company, time is allocated daily for presentations by each SBU to the rest of the participants. Lockheed Martin is a complex organization that was built by acquisition of components from other major corporations, such as IBM, GE, and Martin Marietta. Even a director with over 20 years of experience in the business would not be aware of the activities of the other business units except what could be learned through internal company public relations. There is a considerable amount of internal competition and operational duplication that Lockheed Martin must overcome to remain competitive in the aerospace and defense industry. There are many institutional barriers to collaboration inside the organization at present, and it will take much more than a CEO-level edict claiming that "we are one company" to overcome these internal constraints. The cross-divisional networks that are nurtured by the SLDP are a part of the company's strategy to build more collaboration across the enterprise.

To help you build your network within your organization, the best advice is to take advantage of every opportunity to establish a relationship with a peer in another part of the company. Proactively creating the linkages now will enable you to put the network into action when you need it. Make a point of arranging a lunch meeting once every other week with someone from another unit in your firm. Learn what you can about the business issues other divisions are facing. Seek involvement in task forces that are addressing companywide projects. If you are contacted by someone in another division who is looking for assistance in solving a problem, make "yes" your default response instead of "no."

Demonstrate your willingness to collaborate with other SBUs regardless of the direct benefit to your unit. Developing a reputation as a team player is important. It is even better if you can help other divisions achieve results.

For example, there was a faculty member who wanted to attend a professional meeting that came up at the end of the fiscal year, and his department did not have the funds budgeted to enable his participation. When I learned of his problem, I offered to cover his travel through my unit's budget using the rationale that his professional development was in the best interests of executive education. From this rather simple action I gained a key supporter. I have seen examples over and over again where colleagues refuse to help each other within an organizations. It doesn't make sense to me from both a personal and organizational perspective to be non-collaborative. And it will come back to haunt you!

Case in point: When I moved to the University of South Carolina, the executive education unit was considered an organizational outcast. My predecessor (let's call him Don for the purposes of this example) was a member of the faculty. For reasons that are still not completely clear to me, Don had done his best to alienate everyone in the school. He seemed to go out of his way to make it difficult for other faculty to get involved in the executive education programs. Most of the instructors Don used were outside consultants. The unit was also viewed as noncooperative by other administrative units. Executive education occupied prime office space and had control over the best classrooms in the school. Don and his staff made it clear to all the others in the school who requested use of any of the executive education facility that they should feel fortunate if they were granted access. He was able to get away with his arrogance while the unit was financially successful. But once the economy began to soften and the school had a change in leadership, Don was in jeopardy. The new dean, a fellow faculty member whom Don had treated disrespectfully, worked quickly in targeting executive education for a major overhaul. She pulled together an internal review committee to audit the unit and to recommend changes. Don had no allies and was powerless to withstand the review. He was out within a matter of months. As a tenured faculty member, Don still had a position in the school but no supporters or advocates. In many ways he became a rather pathetic figure inside the organization.

My style (and philosophy) is quite different from Don's. I believe very strongly in the need to work collaboratively and to build strong relationships across the organization. Among my first activities at South Carolina was the establishment of a faculty advisory committee that comprised some of the most influential professors in the school. Rather than creating my own set of policies on faculty involvement in executive education, the advisory committee became the vehicle for creating policy. The chairman of the finance department had told me during the interview process that his faculty had been turned off to executive education due to Don's interactions with them. It did not take long for me to determine that the finance faculty members were among the most powerful in the school, and so I made it a personal mission to regain their participation in executive education. Within one year there were more finance professors teaching in executive education programs than any other department in the school. Toward the end of my work at South Carolina, there was another change in leadership at the school. This time, rather than being susceptible as a target for a new dean, executive education was viewed as a major contributor to the school. There was strong support for the unit's activities among many faculty members, and, as importantly, there were no major enemies waiting to attack.

In today's business climate, everything is fragile and subject to change. The best way to ensure self-preservation is to build positive relationships across the organization. The costs are minimal, in terms of both time and resources, and the potential payoffs are great—both personally and for your division. Build and maintain a dynamic horizontal network of colleagues you can call upon when the need arises. Chances are high that the need will occur sooner rather than later.

QUESTIONS AND EXERCISES

- Can you identify your boss's boss? How could you help your manager look good in that person's eyes?
- Find ways you can provide useful new information or data to your manager. These might include magazine articles, industry analyses, books or courses you have heard about—demonstrate not only that you are interested in your own learning, but also that you want to help your manager pick up key information as well.
- How much do you know about the business challenges other units or divisions face within your company? Make it a point to find out and seek out information from units whose challenges are similar to yours.
- Can you identify the major customers for each SBU? Where is there significant overlap with your unit? How can you leverage resources to optimize marketing activities?
- How are the other units performing? Are there ways in which you can influence the sharing of resources to assist units that are struggling?
- Make a list of the people in the company outside your unit with whom you have a good working relationship. How can you significantly expand that list within the next 6 to 12 months?
- Are there any major divisions in which you have no contacts? How can you correct that?

CHAPTER 13

Managing Across Borders and Cultures

"To manage cultural differences more effectively, the first step in the process is increasing one's general cultural awareness."
—Harris & Moran, *Managing Cultural Differences*

Having been born and raised in the suburbs of New York City and then spending the next 30+ years living in three Southern states, I have an appreciation of the cultural differences in the United States represented by North and South. The consequences of the interaction of the two cultures were amusing as a college student. In business, however, the clashes can have profound impacts on organizational performance. It is not unusual for a manager who is Southern, working with a company headquartered in the Northeast, to be considered an unsophisticated redneck by the "Yankees." Similarly, many Southerners keep the memories of Reconstruction alive in their current perceptions of Northerners—Notherners are not to be trusted and are people with little personal honor. I have seen the results of these types of cultural biases in action.

At Burlington Industries, the marketing and sales force was in New York as part of the fashion industry, while the manufacturing was all in the South (the home of cotton and antiunionism). The marketing-operations interface is a difficult one in most companies, but it was greatly exacerbated at Burlington due to the North-South tension. Similarly, when Maine-based UNUM acquired the South Carolina homegrown company, Colonial Life & Accident Insurance, regionalism was a major factor again in the difficulties that arose between the parent company and the subsidiary. When UNUM eventually began to exercise significant control, the Southerners believed they were reliving the War of Northern

Aggression (as the Civil War is referred to in South Carolina). And executives in Maine did not understand Southern culture well enough to know how to effectively manage organizational integration in this acquisition. The results were less than anticipated returns on capital invested—value leakage—caused to a certain extent by cultural differences within the United States.

If we have this level of difficulty domestically with regard to cross-cultural interactions, imagine what challenges are present for companies that operate across borders and continents. Americans, by and large, are myopic about the world and cultural differences. While U.S. society is considered a "melting pot" of cultures, the boundaries created by two oceans has limited Americans' exposure to how people operate in other cultural settings. That is different from how people from other cultures act when they are trying to adapt to U.S. society. Our lack of sophistication is magnified greatly by the way Americans view foreign languages. We believe everyone speaks, or should speak, English, and so it is not important for our children to learn second or third languages while in primary and secondary school. This is a serious business problem that negatively impacts U.S. companies globally. While English is becoming the global standard for business, managers who are multilingual have a tremendous competitive advantage in both marketing and operations due to their enhanced cultural sensitivity and their ability to communicate with people in their native language.

American naïveté in cross-cultural communications is well documented. While we have made progress from the "ugly American" depictions in the 1960s to a higher level of sophistication, U.S. managers still struggle in working across cultural borders. And the problems are not just language-related.

Case in point: Let's take a deeper view of the American-based research and development unit at Glaxo Pharmaceuticals (prior to the mergers with Burroughs Wellcome and SmithKline Beecham) that was briefly mentioned in Chapter 2. The U.S. group experienced difficulties in working with its British counterparts. Because Glaxo was a British firm, the U.K. side drove Glaxo's R&D activities. The American scientists were frustrated by their seeming lack of influence. They had grown in size and productivity quite unexpectedly due to the huge success of the ulcer medicine, Zantac. It was such a profitable drug in the United States that Glaxo wound up building an extensive R&D facility in North Carolina. Despite their capabilities, the Americans were often shut out of the major decisions for R&D globally. Jim Neidel, then senior vice president for research and development in the United States, explained that one of their problems was the decision-making process employed by the British. According to Neidel, when there was a meeting scheduled in England to make a decision on a major issue, the Americans would show up expecting to have a full discussion that would subsequently result in a collaborative decision. What he and his colleagues discovered is that the meeting was simply a vehicle for announcing the decision that had already been reached. The "discussion" phase was completed long before the meeting was ever held, and it was done covertly behind closed doors. Thus, the Americans never had a chance to influence the decision process since they were not part of these private discussions. The experience reinforced the old adage for Neidel that the United States and United Kingdom were two cultures separated by a common language.

Difficulties resulting from cultural myopia can also arise within an American-based organization that operates on a transnational basis. The Eastman Chemical Company of Kingsport, Tennessee, was expanding its business in Latin America. The managers in the field, primarily expatriates, were increasingly frustrated over the lack of support coming from corporate headquarters. While the company did an adequate job of preparing the managers who were going to work in Latin America about the issues and challenges they (and their families) would face, the executives at corporate headquarters did not have a lot of knowledge of the region. Thus, when the executives were faced with a problem that was related to them by one of their field representatives, they had no frame of reference upon which to base decisions. Their natural inclination was to assume that the circumstances in Latin America were the same as in the United States. This, of course, was not a good assumption, and it left the expatriates without a good line of communication back to the home office. Fortunately, the leadership at Eastman Chemical identified this problem and in 1995 began providing training to their executives on doing business in Latin America. These educational programs were a wise investment, as they greatly increased awareness of the context in which their field managers had to work. Communications between headquarters and the regional offices in Latin America improved considerably.

Xerox faced a related, but slightly different, problem in the communications link between corporate headquarters and the field. The Americas group at Xerox included Canada and the Latin American operations—the United States was in its own division. The company was organized by country, and each major nation operated its own subsidiary with a separate president and board of directors. The Caribbean operated as one entity with a managing director who worked out of headquarters in Connecticut. Brazil was the dominant force, as it was, by far, the most profitable subsidiary. In fact, due to Brazil's success (with help from Mexico), the Americas group was the most profitable division for Xerox worldwide. There was always tension between the country organizations and corporate—and the more power the subsidiary wielded, the higher the tension. Thus, there was considerable angst between Brazil and headquarters. The differences in power also created problems among the subsidiaries. Xerox–Argentina, with the second largest market on the South American continent, was significantly behind Brazil. While Xerox–Chile's organization was advanced, its market was too small to compete with Brazil or Mexico. The cultural differences among the subsidiaries, as well as the difference between them and the U.S. corporate office, made it very difficult to develop a consensus in how to market Xerox products and services throughout the region.

Through the research of my colleagues David Schwieger (South Carolina) and Tugrul Atamer (EM Lyon), it has become increasingly clear that while cultural differences do add significant stress to business performance, these differences do not represent the most important challenge for collaboration across a global enterprise. Where there is agreement on goals and objectives between the parent company (of one culture) and a subsidiary organization (of another culture), cultural differences are surmountable. In fact, they can become a competitive advantage as the cultural diversity enables the company to be more responsive to the local markets. However, where there is no consensus on the basic business goals and objectives, the same cultural differences between parent company and subsidiary can become immovable objects that prevent the organizations from performing collaboratively.

GTE, before its transformation to Verizon, provided a poignant illustration of this point. Last decade, GTE became the largest shareholder of the Venezuelan telephone company and took on its operating responsibilities. GTE struggled for years trying to make that a profitable venture. The classic explanations for the performance problems focused on the cultural differences between the Americans and Venezuelans. The first wave of managers that GTE sent to Caracas had Americans who learned their Spanish and Latin culture in Mexico. They saw Venezuela as simply an eastern extension of Mexico. The GTE expats tried to change the company's operations quickly, without working through the Venezuelan management team that was already in place. And, of course, the Americans concentrated on the technical issues, ignoring the need to first develop good working relationships with their Venezuelan colleagues. Contrast that to GTE's experience in Taiwan, where GTE owned the license to operate cellular phones. The cultural differences between the United States and Taiwan are more profound than between the United States and Venezuela. Certainly, the company was not going to find many, if any, managers within its ranks who knew how to speak Chinese! Yet the company was much more successful in Taiwan. Why? Because the business agendas were aligned in Taiwan. Everybody involved in the organization was in it to build the business. In Venezuela, the local management team was not open to working effectively with the Americans. Similarly, the GTE position on Venezuela was that the phone company there had been failing for quite some time and needed to operate more like a U.S. organization. The personal agendas were significant, and the culture clashes simply became the excuses that each side needed to rationalize its lack of cooperation.

This important lesson has helped me work more effectively with client organizations that operate on a transnational or global basis. It is also a transferable lesson to working across geographic or corporate cultures within the domestic United States as well.

Make sure the groups involved in the business can agree on the fundamental goals and objectives of the organization first before tackling the challenges of cultural diversity. Cross-cultural communication is greatly facilitated when there is alignment on the basic purpose of the enterprise.

A FRAMEWORK FOR ANALYZING CULTURAL DIFFERENCES

There are many ways to look at cultural differences in an organizational context. The individual's orientation to the world is an important component in determining how that person will view other cultures. An ethnocentric orientation, most often associated with Americans, views the world as being similar to the home country. Thus ethnocentrists assume that all people think and act alike, or at least that people from other cultures *should* think and act like the ethnocentrists. In essence, ethnocentrists significantly undervalue the importance of cultural differences in conducting business outside their home country.

The polycentric perspective is one that views every country or culture as completely unique. This orientation operates with the motto of "Think local, act local," where cultural differences become exaggerated and there are few if any opportunities for developing regional economies of scale. In this orientation, cultural differences are overemphasized.

A contrasting orientation is the geocentric perspective, where the individual recognizes similarities and contrasts between and across cultures. Geocentrists neither underestimate nor exaggerate the challenges that cultural differences present in conducting business across national boundaries. It is a world-centered perspective that is important to develop in managers who seek an international business career.

Using a geocentric orientation, the noted Dutch social scientist Geert Hofstede has developed the most widely accepted framework for understanding the organizational impact of cultural differences. His data came from an analysis of cultural differences among groups of employees from different nations who worked for the same global business—IBM. Hofstede identified four principal components to use in comparing and contrasting cultures as means of analyzing the impact of cultural differences on organizations:

1. *Power distance.* Relates to relative gaps of power and influence among the social classes. In cultures that have high power distance, there are large gaps between the haves and have-nots when it comes to career opportunities within business and professional fields. Power distance also refers to the gaps in power and influence within an organizational setting between the executives and middle to frontline managers. In societies that have high power distance, the workers and lower-level managers would be expected to simply follow the orders of the executives without having much empowerment for decision making at their level.

2. *Uncertainty avoidance.* Describes cultural differences related to one's need for structure and one's level of comfort with ambiguity. Cultures that are rated low on uncertainty have nonstructured societies that operate without a high level of formal rules and social norms. Those that are rated high in this dimension reflect people who have a strong need for social order and are uncomfortable with uncertainty.

3. *Individualism-collectivism.* Reflects the continuum of cultures that, on one end, highly value individualism and, on the other end, place a premium on the collectivist needs of the group as a whole.

4. *Masculinity-femininity.* Best defined as the "aggressiveness" versus "softness" of the culture. Societies that are rated high in masculinity value achievement and aggressive behavior in pursuit of goals. Those rated low in this dimension, reflecting more "feministic attributes," value relationships, harmony, and caring for others more than performance.

Hofstede compared each culture against the other 55 countries in the study, thus creating clusters of cultures rated high, medium, and low in each of the four dimensions. The resulting Table 13-1 provides insight into the similarities and differences among 10 of the countries in the study.

T a b l e   13.1

Geert Hofstede's culture comparisons.

Culture Dimension Scores for 10 Countries
PD = power distance; ID = individualism; MA = masculinity; UA = uncertainty
avoidance; LT = long-term orientation
H = top third, M = medium third, L = bottom third (among 53 countries and regions
for the first four dimensions; among 23 countries for the fifth)

	PD	ID	MA	UA	LT
USA	40 L	91 H	62 H	46 L	29
Germany	35 L	67 H	66 H	65 M	31
Japan	54 M	46 M	95 H	92 H	80
France	68 H	71 H	43 M	86 H	30*
Netherlands	38 L	80 H	14 L	53 M	44
Hong Kong	68 H	25 L	57 H	29 L	96
Indonesia	78 H	14 L	46 M	48 L	25*
West Africa	77 H	20 L	46 M	54 M	16
Russia	95*H	50*M	40*L	90*H	10*
China	80*H	20*L	50*M	50*M	118

*Estimated

From this perspective, if we compare France and the United States, we find that the cultures vary most on power distance and uncertainty. China is somewhat similar to the United States only in the area of masculinity, but it has three dimensions in common with France.

Hofstede's framework remains the most-often cited approach to comparing and contrasting cultures. Ronen and Shenkar applied his model to a broad range of countries and identified clusters of cultures that shared similar traits. Figure 13.1 depicts those clusters and illustrates the relative similarities and differences among groups of nations.

In my work with transnational organizations, I have found other factors that are worth considering in analyzing cultural differences in addition to Hofstede's model. These include:

- People's relationship with nature
- Assumptions of humans being inherently good or evil
- Temporal orientation: past, present, and future

F i g u r e   13.1

Ronan and Shenkar country clusters—cultural comparisons.

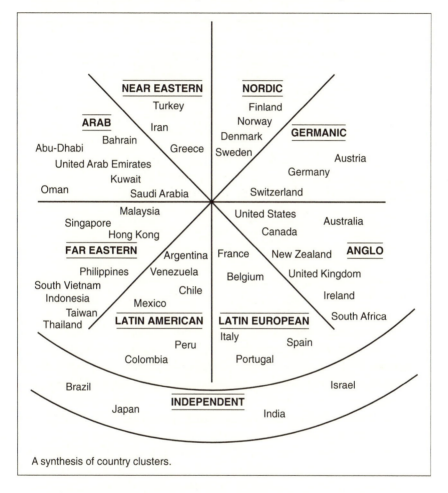

A synthesis of country clusters.

- Personal and family relationships
- Spatial orientation: physical closeness and the need for privacy

To better understand these cross-cultural factors, use the United States as an illustration. Americans believe that people can control nature. We "harness" the wind, use solar power, build hydroelectric dams, and invest significant sums of money in meteorology and related sciences. Americans view humanity as being inherently "good"—we are guided by the principle of "innocent until proven guilty" as a core value in our legal system. We tend to take people at their word and assume the vast majority of our citizens act morally and ethically. In the United States, we live in the present with an eye to the future. The past has little meaning in our culture. We also believe that time is something that has to be managed: "Time is money," "You're wasting my time," and "Time's up" are common expressions in our society. In alignment with the American focus on the present, we are also a youth-oriented culture. We do not honor and respect our elder citizens nearly as much as other cultures. It is less and less common for families to live in multigenerational homes. Rather, Americans are increasingly living in single-parent families. Our friendships tend to operate on a superficial level. Americans are considered genuinely friendly, but only up to a point. Then, it is much harder to get close to someone. This is somewhat related to the vastness of our country, which has built an appreciation for personal (and emotional?) space in our culture. The American dream is to own a big house with a large yard so that each child can have his or her own bedroom and plenty of room to play outdoors. We place a high value on privacy. Many of our yards are fenced in to keep others from invading that privacy. In a corporate context, a symbol of status is to have a private office—the larger, the more power associated with the individual. In interpersonal interactions, our standard is to stand one arm's length away from the person with whom we are talking. It is a sign of intimacy to be closer than that distance with someone. Standing further away would be a sign of disinterest or personal rebuke.

Compare these factors of U.S. society with those characteristic of Arabic cultures. They believe that nature cannot be managed, and so people have to learn to live with nature's forces rather than try to control them. There is a much stronger sense of the basic evilness in humanity among Arab societies that requires more social control, particularly through religion. There is a strong sense of a living past among Arabic cultures. When referring to ancient events, it is common to hear use of the pronoun *we*, not *they*, inferring that people living today were actually a part of that experience and that it is still fresh. Combining these beliefs with a firm belief in fate rather than free will, Arabs are more likely to believe that people cannot influence the future—whatever happens has already been determined. Therefore, their sense of time is quite different from that of Americans. A clock does not "run" in the Middle East—it "walks." Sticking to strict schedules, as with Swiss railroads, is not a part of the Arabic culture. Given their perspective on the past, there is much more reverence for elders than in the United States. Families will likely include all generations in the home. The oldest male is the head of the household, and women in the Middle East play a vastly different role in family life than women in America. There is also a significant difference with regard to personal space between Arabic and Western cultures. Interpersonally, it is common for men to touch each other while conversing. Standing at an arm's length distance from an acquaintance would be insulting to an Arab male. And, in general, there is much less personal privacy than in the United States.

Applying the cultural analysis to a business context, it is clear that the perspective on managerial leadership would be quite different between Americans and Arabs. Strategic planning, for example, would be less relevant to someone from the Middle East due to the heightened sense of determinism. Their view of humanity would make them inclined to carefully control their employees (Theory X) and limit empowerment. Relationships are much more critical to conducting business in Arabic societies than in the United States. It would be important for customer and supplier to become interpersonally acquainted to develop some trust before entering into business agreements. Arabs would honor and pay more attention to the past than to the future in their business dealings. Change would be much slower and problems more likely to be thought of working themselves out in the Middle East than in the United States. These differences are profound, and the sophistication level required to effectively work across these cultures is similarly profound.

MANAGERIAL LEADERSHIP IN THE GLOBAL ENTERPRISE

Cross-cultural sensitivity is a critical quality for managerial leadership today. This concept has been somewhat devalued in the

United States due to the political correctness backlash. Valuing diversity should not be viewed as satisfying federal regulations or preventing minority groups from filing lawsuits. Rather, the goal of managing diversity should be to enable all those in the organization to contribute to their fullest potential by realizing that cultural differences provide valuable contributions to a complex business. Broader perspectives and perceptions about the world offer companies a competitive advantage in serving global markets and competing in multidimensional industries.

In his book *Transcultural Management*, Furakawa identified seven "mental disciplines" that are important in the development of geocentric managers—those individuals who can work effectively across cultures in a global context. These disciplines apply equally as well to managing diversity in domestic settings:

1. *Observe without judgment.* Observation is the key to increasing your understanding of other cultures. However, when we observe, we tend to see through judgmental lenses that immediately characterize each behavior we see as being good or bad. It is important to turn off the judgmental switch when learning how others think. They operate by different norms and social rules that must first be understood before they can be judged.

2. *Tolerate ambiguity.* Societies do not operate in a black and white world; realize that there will be times when behaviors are erratic and rules are unclear. You will find it difficult if you function under the assumption that all people of a certain culture will behave in a consistent fashion.

3. *Practice style shifting.* Similar to the concept of "When in Rome, do as the Romans," you should work on adopting some new behaviors that fit the local culture. When I work in France, I look for ways to alter my lifestyle from the American mindset. For example, I prefer to spend an hour sitting at an outdoor café in the midafternoon rather than driving to a convenience store to grab a coke while running errands. Similarly, I treat meals as more important social events than I do in the States. They are simple changes, per-

haps, but it is helpful in increasing my understanding of French culture.

4. *Flip your perception.* It is certainly true that you cannot really understand other people until you see the world through their eyes. Our perceptions are obviously culturally biased. When you catch yourself making assumptions about another culture, look at the situation from a different angle. If you had been born and raised in that society, how might your perceptions be altered?

5. *Reprogram your questions.* As with the items mentioned above, by challenging your assumptions and culturally biased perceptions, you will begin to seek answers to questions you have not previously considered. You cannot apply Western logic to an issue in an Asian cultural context. To understand how another culture operates, you need to begin thinking as if you were a member of that culture. This is another reason why learning to speak multiple languages is so powerful. When you become fluent in a language, you "think" in that language, which enables you to ask questions that are relevant to that culture, not necessarily to yours.

6. *Work interdependently.* Seek ways in which cultural differences can be leveraged to improve performance. There will be synergistic connections where the whole becomes greater than the sum of its parts when both parties contribute. This may require some sacrifice and compromise, especially at first, in order to find the right platform upon which both parties can effectively interact. This point was made poignantly clear to me by one of my French colleagues, who described his experiences in collaborating with an American peer. They used English as their common language since the American did not have the capability to interact in French. After working together for a few months, the French colleague told the American that he (the Frenchman) will never be able to show how much he truly understands about the topic of their joint research due to his having to communicate in English. While his

language skills were strong, they were not sufficient to communicate complex abstract concepts. This was something he could only do in French. These two individuals have been collaborating on projects for over eight years now and have learned how to minimize this problem through their enhanced knowledge of each other. If the Frenchman had found this too difficult to handle at first, then the good work these two colleagues have accomplished over the years would never have happened. The fact that he was willing to operate on a less-than-level playing field, with the understanding of his American colleague, enabled them to find the interdependence that has helped them both perform at a higher level.

7. *Keep mental stability and growth.* Perhaps it is self-evident that operating across cultures can be challenging and disorienting. I have talked with managers who, as expatriates, have come to adopt much more of the host country culture than their own. And, at the other extreme, I have met Americans who, after working abroad, have become more entrenched in their American orientation and totally rejected the host culture. Living and working outside your home country can be, and should be, a significant learning experience. However, it does require a certain level of emotional maturity and mental stability in order to move across cultural settings.

The geocentric mindset, as proposed by Furakawa, has consistent elements with emotional intelligence, particularly with regard to empathy and self-regulation. Managerial leaders with high EQs are good candidates for working in global enterprises that require cross-cultural understanding and communication. It is a good strategy to provide experience working in different cultural settings for a high-potential manager early in his or her career. For one thing, it is usually less complicated to send younger managers overseas since they are often more flexible in their personal lives than older executives with families and school-age children. More importantly, the lessons learned from this exposure will have multifaceted impact on the individual for years to come. And upon returning to the corporate offices in midcareer, the acquired knowl-edge can be transferred to many more people in the organization than through expatriates who typically come back to the United States at the tail end of their careers.

QUESTIONS AND EXERCISES

- What types of cross-cultural experiences have you had?
- Have you ever been in a situation where you felt like an outsider in another cultural setting for an extended period of time (more than four months)? What lessons did you learn from that experience?
- Categorize the range of ethnic or international cultures that exist within your organization. Which ones are predominant? What are some of the ways in which these cultures clash?
- How could the cultural differences within your organization be better leveraged to enhance performance?
- Are you bilingual? If not, what opportunities does your company or community offer for you to learn a second language?

CHAPTER 14

Putting Your Plan into Action

> *"Even if you're on the right track, you'll get run over if you just sit there."*
>
> —Will Rogers

My congratulations to you, as you must be somewhat motivated to make some behavioral changes in order to enhance your leadership effectiveness or you would not have taken the time to read through this material. You undoubtedly realize that no matter how skilled you are currently, your leadership practices can always be improved and refined. My hope is that this book has helped you think about where you are now and where you want to go with regard to managerial leadership. Of course, thinking about it is the easy part. The challenge lies in the doing—actually changing your leadership behaviors. Unlearning, to me, is much more difficult than learning. Thus, you must be vigilant to the task of breaking old habits that are inconsistent with your desired performance. Simultaneously, you will need to concentrate on learning new skills and techniques to replace those bad habits. Perhaps you began, as many others do, by asking yourself these three questions:

1. *Can you do it?* Absolutely! There is no reason why you should not be able to enhance your leadership practices if you have the true desire to do so.

2. *Will you do it?* Only you can answer this one—as with all personal challenges, either you are committed to it or you're not. There is no middle ground when it comes to this type of behavioral change.

3. *Is it worth it?* Definitely! There are several perspectives to consider in answering this question: the organizational view, your career development, and your personal satisfaction and motivation.

- Look around your organization. Could the company's overall performance be significantly boosted if there was a way to improve leadership effectiveness by 15 percent across the board? Imagine the ripple effects if everyone became more skillful at managing other people. There is no doubt in my mind that the organizational return on investment for leadership development is enormous if executed well.

- From a career perspective, think about the ways in which managers differentiate themselves within a company. What are the major contributing factors to rewards and promotions? The illustrations in Figures 14.1 a–c draw an important picture. If you compared the IQ scores for the middle managers identified as having good potential in a company, you would expect to find a fairly narrow range—somewhere around 110–125 (Figure 14.1a). That does not provide a lot of room for differentiation among the managerial population. If you compared technical knowledge for the same group, instead of IQ, the chances are high that you would find a similar pattern—a range between 1 and 2 standard deviations above the mean, approximately 110–125 (Figure 14.1b). Again, this offers little in terms of distinguishing one manager from another. But if you were to compare EQ scores (or leadership effectiveness ratings) for the same managerial population, there would be a much higher probability for a greater range of scores—perhaps as broad as 75–125 (Figure 14.1c). This (EQ and leadership effectiveness) is often the key differentiator among technically competent,

F i g u r e   14.1a

IQ scores.

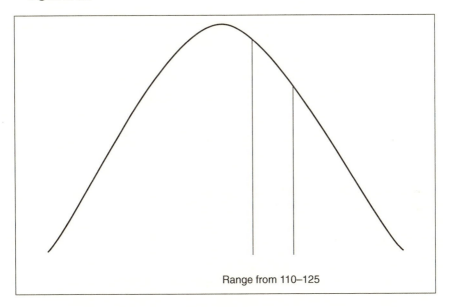

Range from 110–125

reasonably well-educated managers when it comes to promotions and career advancement.

- Most important is the enhanced satisfaction and personal motivation that comes from developing your leadership skills. While I do not wish I could travel back in time to more correctly handle some of the mistakes I made from a leadership perspective, it is very gratifying to realize how much I have learned over the years. Instead of looking backward, that realization has enabled me to take on more and more challenging positions. My heightened self-confidence and belief in the value I provide to my employer increases my level of satisfaction from working—which then enhances my motivation and helps me to keep focusing on my personal growth. Many of the managers whom I have helped work on their leadership development have expressed similar outcomes. There are enormous intrinsic rewards for improving your leadership effectiveness.

Figure 14.1b

Technical competence.

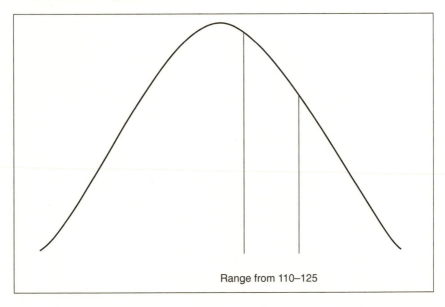

Range from 110–125

This is a journey, not a project. Along the course of the journey you will undoubtedly encounter a variety of situations that will get in the way of your travels or force you to shift directions. Just keep the end destination in mind and, despite the obstacles that get in your way, make sure you somehow continue to move toward that vision. The good news is that there are some steps you can take now to catapult you forward and to minimize the possibilities of getting derailed from your path.

GETTING STARTED

A short preamble before "getting started": I believe in writing things down. Visualizing the words helps me to consider new ideas. The suggestion to start a personal leadership journal sounds hokey, I know, but it can be highly effective. I have done so periodically over the span of my career and wish I had been more disciplined in maintaining a journal. I found it very helpful whenever

F i g u r e   14.1c

EQ score.

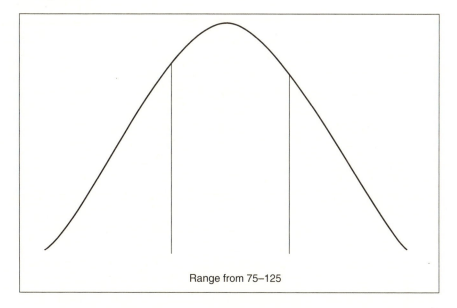

Range from 75–125

I did write down my thoughts and leadership lessons learned—both at the time I made the journal entries and months later upon rereading those pages. If you can overcome the natural disinclination to keep a journal, I strongly encourage you to do so. It would just be for you, no one else. The entries can be as cryptic or as descriptive as you feel appropriate. Your memory will not work well on its own due to all the other noise that infiltrates your brain. If you want to remember a key thought or experience, you will need to capture it somehow. Writing in a journal is the most convenient and personal method.

The critical question to ask is "how" to affect a positive change in your leadership practices. Most of us need some structure in taking on a challenge as important as this one. It is simpler to work from a good model than to create our own. The 10-step approach described below is the most common framework I use in working with managers on their leadership development plans. It is offered as a way for you to get started. Adapt it to fit your needs and your style.

Step 1. The first, and most important, step is to make the commitment to move forward in developing your leadership effectiveness. If you can truly commit yourself to the journey, there are myriad ways to move ahead from that point. Again, I offer you one guiding set of directions, but there are many other approaches to put your plan into action in a way that is most comfortable and meaningful for you.

Step 2. Remember to carefully consider your current situational context. What are the dynamics influencing the industry and the company? Identify the key elements of your organization's culture—both the positives and the negatives. Think about your subordinates and coworkers and the principal issues driving their behaviors. What are the groupings or classifications of note among your associates and how might that affect your leadership behaviors? Paint a complete picture of your organizational environment, including a full description of your followers, peers, and supervisor(s).

Step 3. Collect some data on how others perceive your leadership effectiveness, and be sure to include tools that provide the opportunity for self-assessment. If you have the chance, use a well-validated 360° feedback instrument that addresses leadership practices relevant to your situation. If you do not have access to that type of feedback mechanism, conduct your own survey among key constituency groups. Be sure to keep it anonymous, and structure the questions appropriately to get good-quality feedback. In this way, paint a complete picture of yourself as a managerial leader. Look back at where you have been, and seek a level of understanding of how you have evolved to your present state. What do you see when you look in the mirror?

Step 4: Draw upon the resources available to you within your organization. Suggestions of a few places to look include the company's human resources or organizational development unit. Sometimes, firms have an industrial psychologist on retainer to assist with screening job applicants or promotion candidates. That person may also be able to help you with this process, by either identifying feedback tools or helping you analyze the results. If you do not have any appropriate resources inside the company, seek help from external sources—business schools, independent managerial coaches, or mentors who could assist you in taking a substantive, objective assessment of your current leadership practices.

Step 5: Identify your leadership strengths. What are the skills, abilities, or knowledge you possess that contributes the most to your leadership effectiveness? Use the data you collect to see if others share your perceptions of your best qualities. Those areas in which there is positive consensus among your subordinates, manager, and peers are the most obvious capabilities that work for you. Reflect on how those strengths were developed. Are they a natural part of your personality, or did you learn them through a combination of practical experience and education? Understanding how your best behaviors have developed will help you to learn how you might change your least effective behaviors.

Step 6: Determine the areas in which there are major differences in opinion about your leadership practices. For example, you should take note if your 360° feedback shows that you and your manager rated you highly on "promoting teamwork" but the ratings of your subordinates and peers were more than 1 1/2 points lower (on a 5- or 7-point scale). Gaps of that level on these types of assessment instruments are significant. Some of the items in which you find large rating spreads may be trivial or easily explained. However, most require further investigation. Consider the possible reasons why there are large differences in perspective on a common item. What does this say about your current leadership behaviors?

Step 7: Create your development action plan by identifying two to three areas for improvement initially. There may be more items that require attention, so come up with a staged approach that groups the behaviors in different developmental phases. You can prioritize your list in a variety of ways. First, you should consider behaviors that are currently causing the most damage and that thus need immediate action. You can also pick out some of the "low-hanging fruit"—behaviors that will be relatively easy for you to change and for which you can be reinforced by some quick success. A combination of the two is often the preferred course of action—work on one behavior that will be difficult but is a significant issue for you and a second one that is more easily enhanced so you can begin to see progress right away. Then you can move on to the next item on your list.

Step 8: In identifying these developmental areas, visualize the new behaviors you will exhibit when you are successful. Capture these behavioral descriptions in writing so you can refer to them when necessary. And establish a timetable—how much time should you need to see 35 percent progress, 65 percent progress, or 100 percent progress? How will you know if you have achieved those stages of improvement—what are the milestones you can identify to help you and others see positive change in progress?

As a part of this process, you should determine what types of development activities, if any, you would need to accomplish the improvement you plan to make. This may include educational programs or on-the-job experiences that would assist you in the behavioral change effort.

Step 9: Go public with your action plan. You are much more likely to keep working on your leadership skills if you have told others of your intentions to do so. There are three major elements to this step:

1. Start with your manager. It is an unfortunate reality for most of us that we do not receive regular feedback from our managers about our leadership behaviors. Whatever feedback we do get is concentrated on organizational performance and results. This development process provides you with a terrific platform upon which to have a meaningful dialog with your manager about your managerial leadership capabilities. Go over your 360° feedback profile and clarify any confusing or contradictory data. Then review your development action plan together to make sure you are in agreement about what should be addressed initially and what resources or activities would be available to help you. Review the timetable as well to make sure you both understand when you expect to see progress and what that progress should look like along the way.

2. Make sure you talk with the individuals who gave you feedback—whether through a 360° instrument or from

other assessment tools you employed. First, thank them for taking the time to provide you with their candid feedback. If you ever want to have them give you this kind of information again, you must show them you appreciate their efforts and you plan to do something positive with the data. This also presents you with an opportunity to seek some clarification on their feedback if there were any issues that were difficult to analyze. You definitely do not want to challenge or debate anyone's feedback. Perceptions are what they are. You may disagree, but that does not change the fact that this particular feedback provider has a perception about your behavior that differs from yours.

3. Have a meeting with each of the relevant groups to describe your development action plan and to seek their support. If you have identified "coaching subordinates" as an area that you need to improve, then talk about this in an open meeting with your staff. Ask for their advice on how you might be more effective in coaching them. Try to drill it down to behavioral descriptors rather than only talking in clichéd expressions. If you were to be a better coach to your subordinates, what would they expect to see you do differently? If your peer group is the focus of one of your development items, then make sure to talk with several of them as you would with your subordinates. It is very important that you bring the target audience into your development process. Their input will be instrumental to helping you focus on the appropriate behaviors. And, their support is essential to your success in accomplishing the desired change.

Step 10: Keep your action plan alive. I have worked with many managers who were quite serious about enhancing their leadership practices only to find that desire evaporate over a relatively short period of time. After all, while you may be focused on changing your behaviors, the people around you will function in the same old ways. The corporate culture will not change, nor will your managers behave much differently. There won't be a lot of reinforcement initially for your efforts, but there may be some resentment. Thus, you have to work on self-motivation. Here are five tricks of the trade that can help you avoid the evaporation effect.

1. Physically place your action plan where you will see it regularly. For example, I keep mine in the middle desk drawer. I frequently open this drawer to get pens or paper clips. I do not review the action plan every time I open the drawer, but I am constantly visibly reminded of its existence. If you put the action plan in a file folder that is subsequently put in a file cabinet, it will have a very short half-life. Keep it visible.

2. Find someone who will serve as your "sponsor"—but not your boss, your best friend, or your spouse. It does not have to be someone inside the company, but it could be. Just choose someone you trust who will help remind you of your commitment to the action plan. Give a copy to your sponsor and schedule a date and time for that person to contact you no more than three months out to see how you are progressing.

3. Schedule a second round of feedback using the same assessment instruments you used initially. This should provide you with good comparative pretest-posttest information. You need to give yourself a reasonable amount of time before conducting this follow-up round of feedback in order to work on the behavioral changes. While there is no industry standard, the typical range for the interval between assessments is 9 to 12 months.

4. Build your development efforts into your everyday activities as much as possible. We all complain about not having enough time to get everything accomplished that is asked of us. Thus, adding development activities to the list of things to do is unlikely to happen. Rather than adding more tasks, reframe your current activities to incorporate the items on your action plan. One of the managers at UNUM told me this was a very important concept for him. Delegation and openness to new ideas were two of the items he was addressing in his leadership development plan. He was finding it hard to come up with new activities

that specifically addressed those items. When I suggested he look to his everyday tasks, the solution became apparent. He changed the way he approached his weekly staff meetings by making them more of a forum for discussion than a vehicle for pronouncing his views. And he rotated the responsibility for planning the meetings among his associates as part of his focus on delegation.

5. Be kind to yourself through this difficult process. Reward yourself for the progress you make and do not be too hard on yourself when you regress into old behavioral patterns. You cannot expect to make consistent, steady progress. For every few steps forward, anticipate at least one step back. Just because it seems simple doesn't mean it is easy to accomplish. The important thing is to keep working on it. Your action plan is a dynamic document—review it often and revise it when necessary. Take pleasure in the moments when you notice a positive change in your leadership practices and remain steadfast in your determination to improve when you notice a slip backward.

STAYING ON THE PATH

Remember that this is a journey—one that will last a lifetime. The joy is in the travel and seeing the new sights as you go. My path has been highly rewarding, and simple things can trigger a sense of profound satisfaction. A few years ago, during my time in South Carolina, I was traveling through the Charlotte Airport in North Carolina with a colleague. Just by chance, I ran across an acquaintance, Janet, who had worked with me for a few years at the University of North Carolina. She was traveling with her husband on their way to a prospective job interview. After a brief exchange of pleasantries and catching up on family news, Janet said she enjoyed working for me more than for any other manager for whom she had ever worked. And she just wanted to be sure to thank me for that experience.

We don't realize the impact we have on other people, especially at work. We spend more time (awake) per week with our coworkers than we do with our spouses and children. The interpersonal dynamics we experience on the job have a huge effect on our mental health and well-being. As a "boss," I am constantly amazed at the power of my words among my staff. I can make a statement that was meant as a flip remark, or an off-the-cuff comment, that causes a huge reaction in the office—sometimes for days to come! As managerial leaders, we do not fully appreciate the influence we have over our peers and associates. It is different from the CEO's influence. It is in many ways more powerful than the CEO's influence because it is much more personal.

Case in point: Recently, I was scheduling an overseas trip at a Delta Air Lines ticket office near my home. One of the ticket agents was lightheartedly talking with his colleagues about the "Leo Letter" he had just received congratulating him on his years of service at Delta. I recognized that he was referring to their CEO, Leo Mullin. The agent's colleagues were kidding him by saying that Leo's signature at the bottom of the letter was a stamp, not an original. Some congratulations. The agent was similarly amused and enjoying his colleagues' laughter. After all, Leo Mullin does not have a relationship with this ticket agent and probably never will. But if the agent's direct supervisor had sent him a form letter that was equally impersonal, I am confident the agent would have been upset. And his colleagues would have spoken with him about it without using humor—it would have been a much different conversation.

I do not want to exaggerate my importance to the people with whom I work, but neither do I want to underappreciate it. Every time I am able to improve my leadership effectiveness, it has a positive effect on many other people. The same is true for you. Be the best managerial leader that you can be—for your own sake, for the sake of your colleagues and associates, and for the betterment of your organization. You can make a significant difference.

QUESTIONS AND EXERCISES

- Identify both the organizational and personal resources you can utilize to help you achieve your goals. Think broadly, and ask others to help you determine the company's resources that could be of service to you.
- Identify the organizational barriers that will make it more difficult for you to follow through on your action plan. How can you overcome or work around these barriers?
- Identify the personal barriers or distractions that will make it more difficult for you to follow through on your action plan. Whom can you enlist to help you overcome the barriers to progress that you create?
- Create a dynamic time line for your career path. Start at the point where you first entered the work force as a salaried (exempt) employee. Once you get to your current position, draw your preferred path for the next 5 years, the next 10 years. Where will this lead you? Is this where you want to be in 10 years? How will enhancing your leadership effectiveness help you get where you want to go?
- Identify at least one leadership development activity you will experience this year (in addition to reading this book). What do you need to do in order to make sure you get that experience?

APPENDIX A

Bibliography and Suggested Readings

Auerbach, Red, and Ken Dooley. *MBA: Management by Auerbach.*

Bennis, Warren, and Burt Nanus. *Leaders: The Strategies for Taking Charge.* New York: Harper & Row, 1985.

Blanchard, Ken. *How Leaders Lead.* 1995.

———, and Spencer Johnson. *The One Minute Manager.* 1993.

Collins, James. "Level 5 Leadership." *Harvard Business Review*, Vol. 79, No. 1, January 2001, pp. 66–76.**

———, and Jerry I. Porras. *Built to Last.* New York: Harper-Business, 1997.

Covey, Stephen R. *The Seven Habits of Highly Effective People.* New York: Fireside, 1990.

Drucker, Peter. *The Practice of Management.*

Furakawa, Atsushi. *Transcultural Management.* San Fransisco: Jossey-Bass, 1997.

Goleman, Daniel. *Emotional Intelligence.* New York: Bantam Books, 1995.

———. "What Makes a Leader?" *Harvard Business Review*, 1998.**

Herzberg, Frederick. *The Motivation to Work.* 1959.**

Hofstede, Geert. *Cultures and Organizations: Software of the Mind*, rev. ed. London: McGraw-Hill, 1997.**

Homer. *The Odyssey*, translated by Robert Fitzgerald. Noonday Press, 1998.

Kohlberg, Lawrence. *Essays on Moral Development.* San Fransisco: Harper & Row, 1981.

Kotter, John. *The Leadership Factor.* New York: Free Press, 1988.

Kouzes, James, and Barry Possner. *The Leadership Challenge.* San Fransisco: Jossey-Bass, 1996.**

MacKenzie, Gordon. *Orbiting the Giant Hairball.* New York: Viking Press, 1996.

Maslow, Abraham. *Toward a Psychology of Being*, 2nd ed. New York: Van Nostrand, 1968.

Moran, Robert T. *Managing Cultural Differences.* Gulf Publishing, 1988.

National Commission on Teaching and America's Future. *What Matters Most: Teaching for America's Future.* Commission Final Report, 1996.

"The New Post-Heroic Leadership." *Fortune*, cover story. February 21, 1994.**

Peters, Tom. *In Search of Excellence.* San Fransisco: Warner Books, 1988.**

**This reference is a highly recommended reading.

Roberts, Wess. *Leadership Secrets of Attila the Hun*. New York: Warner
    Books, 1991.
Ronen, S., and Oded Shenkar. "Clustering Variables: The Application of Non
    Metric Multivariate Analysis Techniques in Comparative Management
    Research." *International Studies of Management and Organization*,
    Vol.28, No.3, Fall 1988, pp. 72–78.
Roper Starch Worldwide. *Employee Review: Insights into Workforce Attitudes*.
    Research report sponsored by Randstad North America, 2000.
Slater, Robert. *The GE Way Fieldbook*. New York: McGraw-Hill, 2000.
Smith, Dean E., with John Kilgo and Sally Jenkins. *A Coach's Life*. New York:
    Random House, 1999.**
Tichy, N., and Ram Charan. "Speed, Simplicity, Self-Confidence." *Harvard
    Business Review* reprint No. 89513, September–October 1989.**

**This reference is highly recommended reading.

Samples of 360° Feedback Profiles

LEAD Report: Introduction

The LEAD Survey is a multi-rater survey that provides the participant with feedback about his or her management and leadership competencies. The competencies identified are the underlying characteristics that have been shown to cause or predict outstanding job performance. Competencies include skills and knowledge, as well as social role, self-image, traits, and motives. The instrument focuses upon the competencies necessary for achieving personal and organizational objectives that are critical for success in a changing managerial environment.

Research has shown that as individuals become more aware of strengths and needs they can better plan their career development strategy. When used in conjunction with the accompanying GUIDE TO DEVELOPMENT, the information in this report can be a valuable tool for evaluating perceptions and for creating competency development objectives – with action steps – which will make a difference in job performance and in positive perceptions of work associates.

Reviewing this feedback by analyzing the findings is the beginning of the process. As you work with a coach who is experienced in feedback analysis and developmental learning, you will find that opportunities for growth are numerous and rewarding.

This report is organized into five primary sections:

- LEAD Report Introduction
- LEAD Job Priorities
- Performance on Competency Dimensions
- Performance on Competency Dimensions' Sub-categories
- Performance on Survey Items by Competency

"We are measured not by what we are,
but by the perceptions of what we seem to be;
Not by what we say, but how we are heard;
And not by what we do, but how we appear to do it."

189

Notes on Reading Charts

The sample chart below indicates the data points and symbols for all observers. The X for peers and O for reports are placed at the point of the average of their scores. Boss and self scores are reported individually. Refer to the legend at the bottom of the page for an explanation of the rating scale.

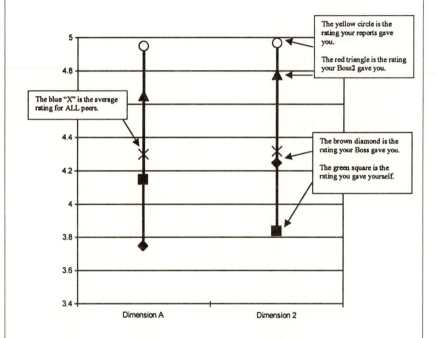

The yellow circle is the rating your reports gave you.

The red triangle is the rating your Boss2 gave you.

The blue "X" is the average rating for ALL peers.

The brown diamond is the rating your Boss gave you.

The green square is the rating you gave yourself.

Ratings given on the survey were as follows:
  Strongly disagree (Not at all to a very small extent) = 1
  Disagree (Between very low to average) = 2
  Neither Agree nor Disagree (Average to normal degree) = 3
  Agree (Between slightly above average to very high) = 4
  Strongly Agree (Very high extent to always) = 5
  Not Applicable (No opportunity to see this demonstrated) = 6

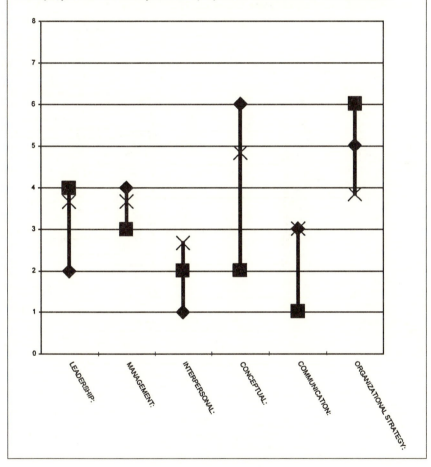

LEAD Job Priorities

All respondents to the survey were asked to rank the importance of each of the Leadership Competency Dimensions - the characteristics that may describe an effective leader. These rankings help you see differences and similarities in what you, your boss and all others perceive as very important (1-4), and important (5-8) for your position.

Performance on Competency Dimensions

This chart provides you with an overall perspective by showing you the average scores you and all other raters gave on the competency dimensions. This information includes the average score of all statements related to each competency dimension and shows you how your self-perceptions compare to the perceptions of others regarding how you demonstrate these work competencies.

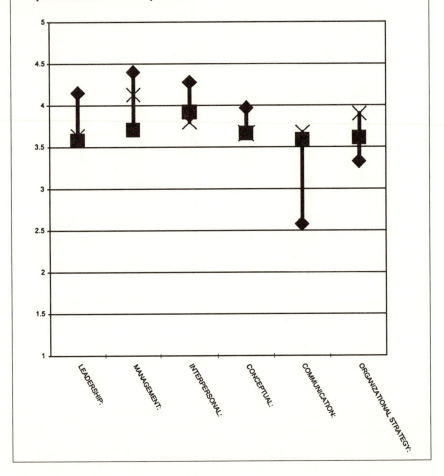

Performance on Competency Dimensions' Sub-categories

Each of the competency dimensions has several specific competencies listed below them. For each of the subcategories (specific competencies), you are given the average scores of all raters for the Survey items which pertain to that specific competency. The information on these pages can help you focus upon specific competencies where perceptions were most and least similar.

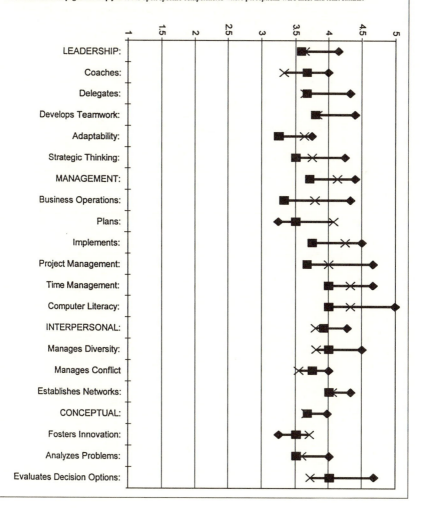

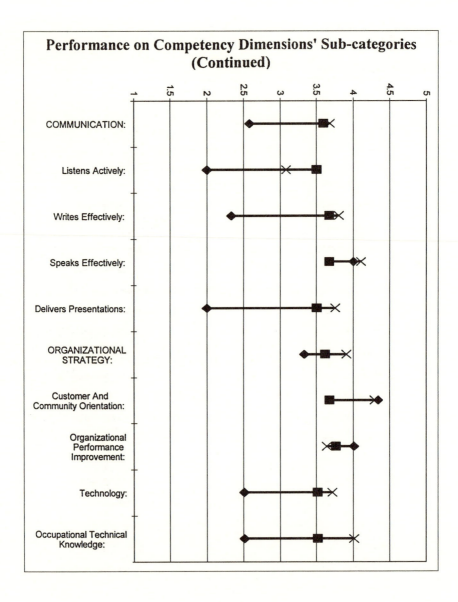

Performance on Competency Dimensions' Sub-categories (Continued)

Performance on Survey Items by Competency

Items on the Survey were attributes and qualities that raters were asked to evaluate. Self and others based their choices, Strongly Disagree (1) to Strongly Agree (5), upon the extent to which the participant is seen demonstrating the behavior.

Survey Items	Self	Boss	Peers
LEADERSHIP:	3.58	4.15	3.64
Coaches:	3.67	4	3.33
Strives to help others find ways to improve their performance	3	3	3.17
Demonstrates a commitment to the development of others	4	5	3.5
Offers support and counsel to assist others in their career advancement	4	4	3.33
Delegates:	3.67	4.33	3.64
Delegates appropriate amounts of tasks and responsibilities to subordinates	4	5	4.5
Lets others learn from mistakes through effective feedback	4	4	2.6
Empowers others by establishing guidelines and defining resources	3	4	3.83
Develops Teamwork:	3.8	4.4	3.83
Helps individuals identify their best means of contributing to team success	4	5	3.33
Encourages cooperation and collaboration in the group	4	5	4
Guides the team to link its work with the strategies of the organization	3	4	4
Encourages the group to gather information needed to make good decisions	4	4	4.17
Shows a commitment to the success of others	4	4	3.67
Adaptability:	3.25	3.75	3.63
Sees failures and mistakes as opportunities for improvement	2	3	3.33
Initiates changes to achieve strategic objectives	4	4	3.6
Anticipates the need to develop change initiatives before they are necessary	3	3	3.2
Maintains an awareness of how changes can impact the organization's vision	4	5	4.4
Strategic Thinking:	3.5	4.25	3.75
Visualizes what changes will move the organization forward in the future	3	5	3.67
Shows foresight by anticipating and planning for environmental changes	3	4	3.5
Has a clear notion of the future direction and needs of the organization	4	4	4
Is committed to implementing the organization's vision on a day-to-day basis	4	4	3.83
MANAGEMENT:	3.71	4.4	4.13
Business Operations:	3.33	4.33	3.79
Knows and understands the internal business operations	3	4	4.33
Demonstrates an understanding of how the organization is run	4	5	4.17
Is quick to respond when external business issues can impact the organization	4	5	4.17
Uses a knowledge of market and environmental trends when making decisions	2	4	3.4
Is quick to address difficult employee situations	4	5	3.17
Uses and communicates financial information to manage effectively	3	3	3.5
Plans:	3.5	3.25	4.07
Creates dialogue regarding goals and objectives with the group to ensure clarity	4	3	4.33
Considers time and resources required when establishing goals	4	2	4.17
Sets realistic estimates of human and physical resources needed when planning	3	4	3.6
Plans and organizes work in a systematic manner	3	4	4.17
Implements:	3.75	4.5	4.25
Gets things done through effective use of resources	3	4	4.33
Takes corrective actions and modifies plans to get the best results possible	4	5	4
Has the insight to see what needs to be done and does it	4	4	4.33
Maintains a commitment to meeting project goals in the face of obstacles	4	5	4.33
Project Management:	3.67	4.67	4
Adapts unique strategies to get things done	4	4	3.67
Sets clear and appropriate timelines to achieve project goals	4	5	4
Manages work processes effectively and efficiently	3	5	4.33
Time Management:	4	4.67	4.33

Survey Items	Self	Boss	Peers
Is concerned about getting things done on time	4	5	4.67
Insists that things get completed when they are promised	5	5	4.33
Has objectives which are time specific and measurable	3	4	4
Computer Literacy:	4	5	4.33
Has sufficient computer skills to function efficiently in the organization	4	5	4.5
Is proficient in computer applications appropriate to work responsibilities	4	5	4.5
Uses available computer resources to get the job done	4	5	4
INTERPERSONAL:	3.92	4.28	3.8
Manages Diversity:	4	4.5	3.81
Is able to work with others from diverse backgrounds	4	5	3.83
Creates an atmosphere of inclusiveness in the work environment	4	4	3.8
Manages Conflict	3.75	4	3.54
Anticipates and deals with problems before they become unmanageable	4	4	3.5
Is sensitive to internal dynamics of the organization	4	3	3.83
Works to quickly resolve conflicts by acting objectively and decisively	4	4	3.5
Shows confidence and composure when dealing with challenges and ambiguities	3	5	3.33
Establishes Networks:	4	4.33	4.05
Teams up well with internal and external people to get things done	4	5	4.33
Engages colleagues inside and outside the organization to exchange information	4	4	3.83
Networks internally and externally to seek advice and support	4	4	4
CONCEPTUAL:	3.67	3.97	3.66
Fosters Innovation:	3.5	3.25	3.7
Encourages the use of creative ideas of others in an effective manner	3	4	3.8
Looks for promising ideas and takes the necessary risks to try them	4	3	3.67
Generates new concepts and ideas that are not apparent to others	3	3	3.67
Creates unique and leading-edge ideas to enhance organizational performance	4	3	3.67
Analyzes Problems:	3.5	4	3.58
Studies all information about a problem and discerns what is important	4	4	3.5
Focuses on relevant details while keeping a big picture perspective	3	4	3.5
Is able to understand what is most important when dealing with complex issues	3	4	3.5
Draws sound conclusions by assessing relevant information	4	4	3.83
Evaluates Decision Options:	4	4.67	3.71
Strives to make balanced decisions even when there are competing priorities	4	4	3.67
Uses adequate information and alternative solutions to make sound decisions	4	5	3.67
Considers consequences of various options and chooses the best alternatives	4	5	3.8
COMMUNICATION:	3.59	2.58	3.68
Listens Actively:	3.5	2	3.08
Takes time to reflect upon what someone is saying before responding	3	2	2.83
Makes a conscious effort not to interrupt others	4	2	3.33
Writes Effectively:	3.67	2.33	3.8
Effectively and clearly presents ideas in written form	4	2	3.5
Concisely writes technical information in an understandable manner	3	2	3.4
Is able to present written information in understandable language	4	3	4.5
Speaks Effectively:	3.67	4	4.1
Uses clear and concise language when speaking	3	5	4.33
Presents ideas in a logical way where the point is clear when speaking	4	5	4.17
Prepares and presents effective speeches appropriate to the topic announced	4	2	3.8
Delivers Presentations:	3.5	2	3.75
Designs presentations that reach every level of understanding in the group	3	2	3.5
Effectively presents information in a natural manner	4	2	4
ORGANIZATIONAL STRATEGY:	3.61	3.33	3.9
Customer And Community Orientation:	3.67	4.33	4.28
Demonstrates an interest in receiving customers' input about products/services	4	4	4.33
Anticipates the effect of important decisions on internal and external customers	3	4	4
Strives to meet and exceed customers' expectations	4	5	4.5

Survey Items	Self	Boss	Peers
Organizational Performance Improvement:	3.75	4	3.63
Uses a systematic approach in planning, monitoring, and improving processes	3	3	3.5
Practices performance improvements methods in day-to-day work situations	4	5	3.4
Understands and applies performance improvement methods to achieve goals	3	3	3.8
Works to ensure seamless delivery of services to internal and external customers	5	5	3.83
Technology:	3.5	2.5	3.7
Stays informed about new technology developments in their field	3	2	3.83
Presents ideas about new technical information for use in the organization	3	2	3.33
Adopts new technology which can promote organizational performance	4	3	3.83
Demonstrates a working knowledge of current technology and applications	4	3	3.8
Occupational Technical Knowledge:	3.5	2.5	3.99
Maintains a high level of competency in occupational technical areas of his/her job	3	2	4.17
Is thoroughly familiar with new industry developments, policies, and practices	4	3	3.5
Shows a high level of expertise in their technical area	3	3	4.5
Researches technical information about ideas and practices in their field	4	2	3.8

LEAD Report:
Introduction

The LEAD Survey is a multi-rater survey that provides the participant with feedback about his or her management and leadership competencies. The competencies identified are the underlying characteristics that have been shown to cause or predict outstanding job performance. Competencies include skills and knowledge, as well as social role, self-image, traits, and motives. The instrument focuses upon the competencies necessary for achieving personal and organizational objectives that are critical for success in a changing managerial environment.

Research has shown that as individuals become more aware of strengths and needs they can better plan their career development strategy. When used in conjunction with the accompanying GUIDE TO DEVELOPMENT, the information in this report can be a valuable tool for evaluating perceptions and for creating competency development objectives – with action steps – which will make a difference in job performance and in positive perceptions of work associates.

Reviewing this feedback by analyzing the findings is the beginning of the process. As you work with a coach who is experienced in feedback analysis and developmental learning, you will find that opportunities for growth are numerous and rewarding.

This report is organized into five primary sections:

- LEAD Report Introduction
- LEAD Job Priorities
- Performance on Competency Dimensions
- Performance on Competency Dimensions' Sub-categories
- Performance on Survey Items by Competency

"We are measured not by what we are,
but by the perceptions of what we seem to be;
Not by what we say, but how we are heard;
And not by what we do, but how we appear to do it."

Notes on Reading Charts

The sample chart below indicates the data points and symbols for all observers. The X for peers and O for reports are placed at the point of the average of their scores. Boss and self scores are reported individually. Refer to the legend at the bottom of the page for an explanation of the rating scale.

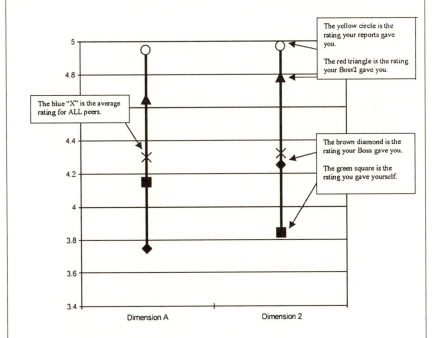

The yellow circle is the rating your reports gave you.

The red triangle is the rating your Boss2 gave you.

The blue "X" is the average rating for ALL peers.

The brown diamond is the rating your Boss gave you.

The green square is the rating you gave yourself.

Ratings given on the survey were as follows:
   Strongly disagree (Not at all to a very small extent) = 1
   Disagree (Between very low to average) = 2
   Neither Agree nor Disagree (Average to normal degree) = 3
   Agree (Between slightly above average to very high) = 4
   Strongly Agree (Very high extent to always) = 5
   Not Applicable (No opportunity to see this demonstrated) = 6

LEAD Job Priorities

All respondents to the survey were asked to rank the importance of each of the Leadership Competency Dimensions - the characteristics that may describe an effective leader. These rankings help you see differences and similarities in what you, your boss and all others perceive as very important (1-4), and important (5-8) for your position.

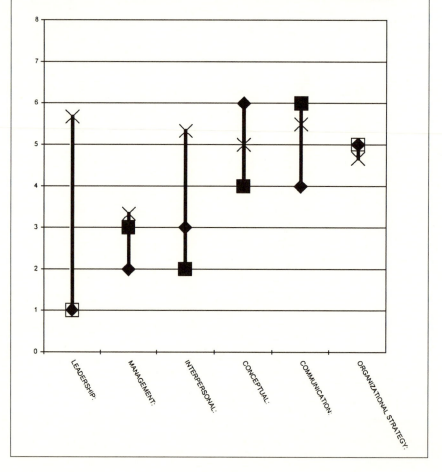

Performance on Competency Dimensions

This chart provides you with an overall perspective by showing you the average scores you and all other raters gave on the competency dimensions. This information includes the average score of all statements related to each competency dimension and shows you how your self-perceptions compare to the perceptions of others regarding how you demonstrate these work competencies.

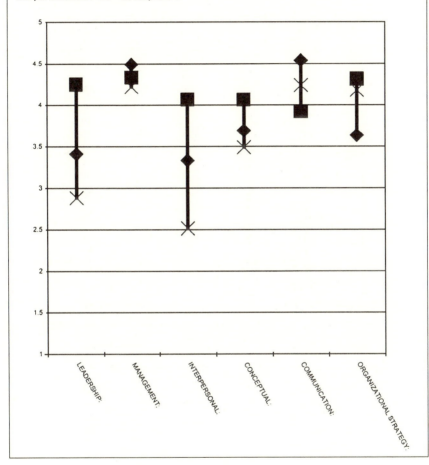

Performance on Competency Dimensions' Sub-categories

Each of the competency dimensions has several specific competencies listed below them. For each of the subcategories (specific competencies), you are given the average scores of all raters for the Survey items which pertain to that specific competency. The information on these pages can help you focus upon specific competencies where perceptions were most and least similar.

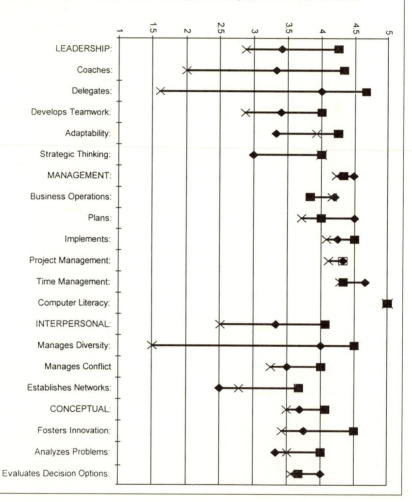

Performance on Competency Dimensions' Sub-categories (Continued)

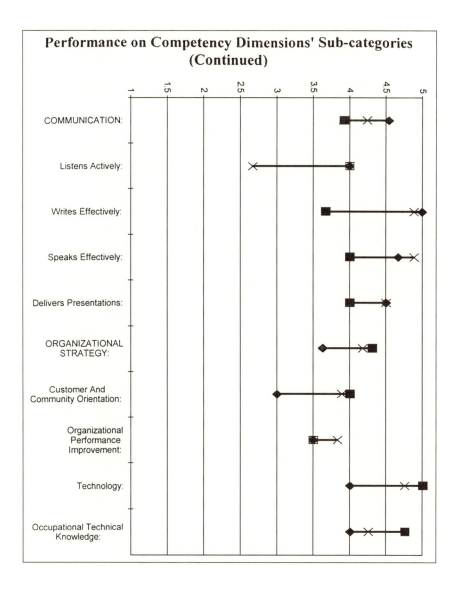

Performance on Survey Items by Competency

Items on the Survey were attributes and qualities that raters were asked to evaluate. Self and others based their choices, Strongly Disagree (1) to Strongly Agree (5), upon the extent to which the participant is seen demonstrating the behavior.

Survey Items	Self	Boss	Peers
LEADERSHIP:	4.25	3.41	2.88
Coaches:	4.33	3.33	2
Strives to help others find ways to improve their performance	4	4	2.33
Demonstrates a commitment to the development of others	4	3	2.67
Offers support and counsel to assist others in their career advancement	5	3	1
Delegates:	4.67	4	1.61
Delegates appropriate amounts of tasks and responsibilities to subordinates	4	4	1.5
Lets others learn from mistakes through effective feedback	5	4	1
Empowers others by establishing guidelines and defining resources	5	4	2.33
Develops Teamwork:	4	3.4	2.87
Helps individuals identify their best means of contributing to team success	4	4	2.33
Encourages cooperation and collaboration in the group	4	4	2.33
Guides the team to link its work with the strategies of the organization	4	4	3.67
Encourages the group to gather information needed to make good decisions	4	2	3.67
Shows a commitment to the success of others	4	3	2.33
Adaptability:	4.25	3.33	3.92
Sees failures and mistakes as opportunities for improvement	5	3	3
Initiates changes to achieve strategic objectives	4	4	5
Anticipates the need to develop change initiatives before they are necessary	4	3	4
Maintains an awareness of how changes can impact the organization's vision	4	6	3.67
Strategic Thinking:	4	3	4
Visualizes what changes will move the organization forward in the future	4	4	4
Shows foresight by anticipating and planning for environmental changes	3	6	4
Has a clear notion of the future direction and needs of the organization	5	2	3.67
Is committed to implementing the organization's vision on a day-to-day basis	4	6	4.33
MANAGEMENT:	4.33	4.49	4.22
Business Operations:	3.83	4.2	4.16
Knows and understands the internal business operations	4	5	4.33
Demonstrates an understanding of how the organization is run	5	4	4.33
Is quick to respond when external business issues can impact the organization	3	4	4
Uses a knowledge of market and environmental trends when making decisions	4	4	4.33
Is quick to address difficult employee situations	3	4	4
Uses and communicates financial information to manage effectively	4	6	4
Plans:	4	4.5	3.71
Creates dialogue regarding goals and objectives with the group to ensure clarity	4	4	4
Considers time and resources required when establishing goals	4	4	3.5
Sets realistic estimates of human and physical resources needed when planning	4	5	3
Plans and organizes work in a systematic manner	4	5	4.33
Implements:	4.5	4.25	4.08
Gets things done through effective use of resources	5	5	4
Takes corrective actions and modifies plans to get the best results possible	4	4	4
Has the insight to see what needs to be done and does it	5	4	4
Maintains a commitment to meeting project goals in the face of obstacles	4	4	4.33
Project Management:	4.33	4.33	4.11
Adapts unique strategies to get things done	5	4	4.67
Sets clear and appropriate timelines to achieve project goals	4	5	4
Manages work processes effectively and efficiently	4	4	3.67
Time Management:	4.33	4.67	4.28

Survey Items	Self	Boss	Peers
Is concerned about getting things done on time	5	5	4.33
Insists that things get completed when they are promised	4	4	4.5
Has objectives which are time specific and measurable	4	5	4
Computer Literacy:	5	5	5
Has sufficient computer skills to function efficiently in the organization	5	5	5
Is proficient in computer applications appropriate to work responsibilities	5	5	5
Uses available computer resources to get the job done	5	5	5
INTERPERSONAL:	4.06	3.33	2.51
Manages Diversity:	4.5	4	1.5
Is able to work with others from diverse backgrounds	4	4	2
Creates an atmosphere of inclusiveness in the work environment	5	6	1
Manages Conflict	4	3.5	3.25
Anticipates and deals with problems before they become unmanageable	4	5	3
Is sensitive to internal dynamics of the organization	4	4	3
Works to quickly resolve conflicts by acting objectively and decisively	4	3	3.33
Shows confidence and composure when dealing with challenges and ambiguities	4	2	3.67
Establishes Networks:	3.67	2.5	2.78
Teams up well with internal and external people to get things done	4	3	2
Engages colleagues inside and outside the organization to exchange information	4	6	3.33
Networks internally and externally to seek advice and support	3	2	3
CONCEPTUAL:	4.06	3.69	3.49
Fosters Innovation:	4.5	3.75	3.42
Encourages the use of creative ideas of others in an effective manner	5	4	2
Looks for promising ideas and takes the necessary risks to try them	4	4	4
Generates new concepts and ideas that are not apparent to others	4	3	3.67
Creates unique and leading-edge ideas to enhance organizational performance	5	4	4
Analyzes Problems:	4	3.33	3.5
Studies all information about a problem and discerns what is important	4	3	3.67
Focuses on relevant details while keeping a big picture perspective	4	6	3
Is able to understand what is most important when dealing with complex issues	4	4	4.33
Draws sound conclusions by assessing relevant information	4	3	3
Evaluates Decision Options:	3.67	4	3.56
Strives to make balanced decisions even when there are competing priorities	4	4	3.67
Uses adequate information and alternative solutions to make sound decisions	4	4	3.67
Considers consequences of various options and chooses the best alternatives	3	4	3.33
COMMUNICATION:	3.92	4.54	4.24
Listens Actively:	4	4	2.67
Takes time to reflect upon what someone is saying before responding	4	3	2.67
Makes a conscious effort not to interrupt others	4	5	2.67
Writes Effectively:	3.67	5	4.89
Effectively and clearly presents ideas in written form	4	5	4.67
Concisely writes technical information in an understandable manner	3	6	5
Is able to present written information in understandable language	4	5	5
Speaks Effectively:	4	4.67	4.89
Uses clear and concise language when speaking	4	5	4.67
Presents ideas in a logical way where the point is clear when speaking	4	4	5
Prepares and presents effective speeches appropriate to the topic announced	4	5	5
Delivers Presentations:	4	4.5	4.5
Designs presentations that reach every level of understanding in the group	4	5	4.33
Effectively presents information in a natural manner	4	4	4.67
ORGANIZATIONAL STRATEGY:	4.31	3.63	4.18
Customer And Community Orientation:	4	3	3.89
Demonstrates an interest in receiving customers' input about products/services	4	2	4
Anticipates the effect of important decisions on internal and external customers	4	3	3
Strives to meet and exceed customers' expectations	4	4	4.67

Survey Items	Self	Boss	Peers
Organizational Performance Improvement:	3.5	3.5	3.83
Uses a systematic approach in planning, monitoring, and improving processes	4	6	4
Practices performance improvements methods in day-to-day work situations	3	6	4
Understands and applies performance improvement methods to achieve goals	3	3	3.33
Works to ensure seamless delivery of services to internal and external customers	4	4	4
Technology:	5	4	4.75
Stays informed about new technology developments in their field	5	4	4.67
Presents ideas about new technical information for use in the organization	5	3	4.33
Adopts new technology which can promote organizational performance	5	5	5
Demonstrates a working knowledge of current technology and applications	5	4	5
Occupational Technical Knowledge:	4.75	4	4.25
Maintains a high level of competency in occupational technical areas of his/her job	5	6	4.67
Is thoroughly familiar with new industry developments, policies, and practices	5	5	3.67
Shows a high level of expertise in their technical area	4	6	4.33
Researches technical information about ideas and practices in their field	5	3	4.33

LEAD Report:
Introduction

The LEAD Survey is a multi-rater survey that provides the participant with feedback about his or her management and leadership competencies. The competencies identified are the underlying characteristics that have been shown to cause or predict outstanding job performance. Competencies include skills and knowledge, as well as social role, self-image, traits, and motives. The instrument focuses upon the competencies necessary for achieving personal and organizational objectives that are critical for success in a changing managerial environment.

Research has shown that as individuals become more aware of strengths and needs they can better plan their career development strategy. When used in conjunction with the accompanying GUIDE TO DEVELOPMENT, the information in this report can be a valuable tool for evaluating perceptions and for creating competency development objectives – with action steps – which will make a difference in job performance and in positive perceptions of work associates.

Reviewing this feedback by analyzing the findings is the beginning of the process. As you work with a coach who is experienced in feedback analysis and developmental learning, you will find that opportunities for growth are numerous and rewarding.

This report is organized into five primary sections:

- LEAD Report Introduction
- LEAD Job Priorities
- Performance on Competency Dimensions
- Performance on Competency Dimensions' Sub-categories
- Performance on Survey Items by Competency

"We are measured not by what we are,
but by the perceptions of what we seem to be;
Not by what we say, but how we are heard;
And not by what we do, but how we appear to do it."

Notes on Reading Charts

The sample chart below indicates the data points and symbols for all observers. The X for peers and O for reports are placed at the point of the average of their scores. Boss and self scores are reported individually. Refer to the legend at the bottom of the page for an explanation of the rating scale.

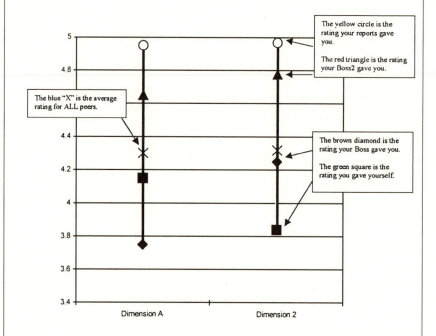

Ratings given on the survey were as follows:

   Strongly disagree (Not at all to a very small extent) = 1
   Disagree (Between very low to average) = 2
   Neither Agree nor Disagree (Average to normal degree) = 3
   Agree (Between slightly above average to very high) = 4
   Strongly Agree (Very high extent to always) = 5
   Not Applicable (No opportunity to see this demonstrated) = 6

LEAD Job Priorities

All respondents to the survey were asked to rank the importance of each of the Leadership Competency Dimensions - the characteristics that may describe an effective leader. These rankings help you see differences and similarities in what you, your boss and all others perceive as very important (1-4), and important (5-8) for your position.

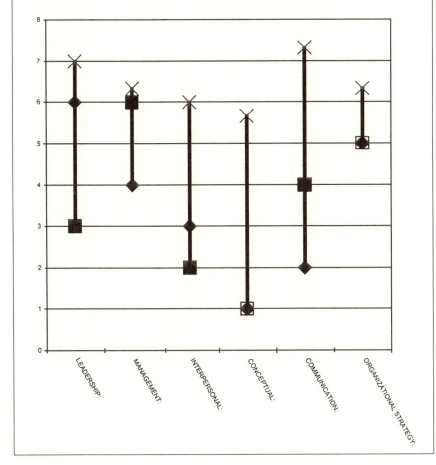

Performance on Competency Dimensions

This chart provides you with an overall perspective by showing you the average scores you and all other raters gave on the competency dimensions. This information includes the average score of all statements related to each competency dimension and shows you how your self-perceptions compare to the perceptions of others regarding how you demonstrate these work competencies.

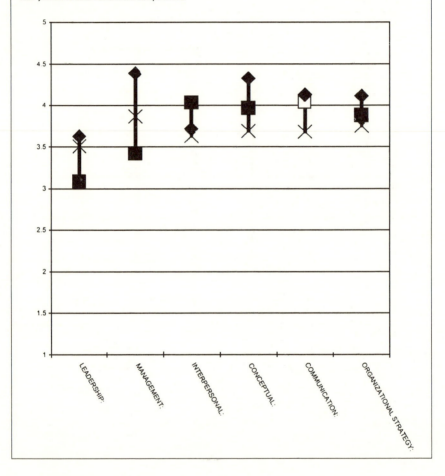

Performance on Competency Dimensions' Sub-categories

Each of the competency dimensions has several specific competencies listed below them. For each of the subcategories (specific competencies), you are given the average scores of all raters for the Survey items which pertain to that specific competency. The information on these pages can help you focus upon specific competencies where perceptions were most and least similar.

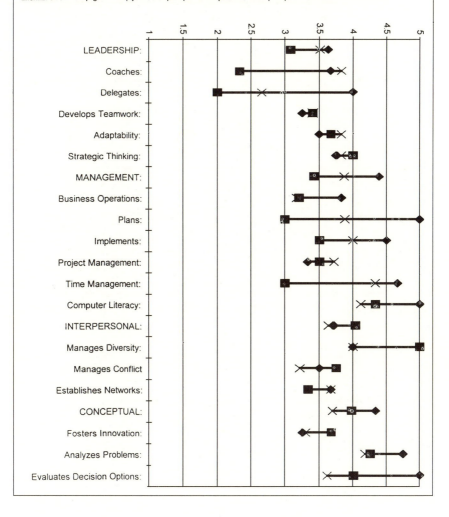

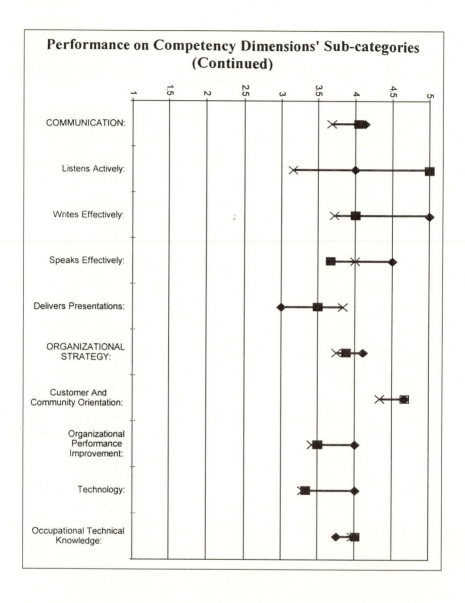

Performance on Competency Dimensions' Sub-categories (Continued)

Performance on Survey Items by Competency

Items on the Survey were attributes and qualities that raters were asked to evaluate. Self and others based their choices, Strongly Disagree (1) to Strongly Agree (5), upon the extent to which the participant is seen demonstrating the behavior.

Survey Items	Self	Boss	Peers
LEADERSHIP:	3.08	3.63	3.51
Coaches:	2.33	3.67	3.83
Strives to help others find ways to improve their performance	2	4	4
Demonstrates a commitment to the development of others	2	4	4
Offers support and counsel to assist others in their career advancement	3	3	3.5
Delegates:	2	4	2.66
Delegates appropriate amounts of tasks and responsibilities to subordinates	6	6	6
Lets others learn from mistakes through effective feedback	2	4	3.33
Empowers others by establishing guidelines and defining resources	6	6	2
Develops Teamwork:	3.4	3.25	3.4
Helps individuals identify their best means of contributing to team success	4	3	3.67
Encourages cooperation and collaboration in the group	4	3	4
Guides the team to link its work with the strategies of the organization	3	6	3
Encourages the group to gather information needed to make good decisions	3	4	3.33
Shows a commitment to the success of others	3	3	3
Adaptability:	3.67	3.5	3.83
Sees failures and mistakes as opportunities for improvement	4	3	4.33
Initiates changes to achieve strategic objectives	3	4	4
Anticipates the need to develop change initiatives before they are necessary	6	3	3
Maintains an awareness of how changes can impact the organization's vision	4	4	4
Strategic Thinking:	4	3.75	3.83
Visualizes what changes will move the organization forward in the future	6	3	4
Shows foresight by anticipating and planning for environmental changes	6	3	3
Has a clear notion of the future direction and needs of the organization	4	4	4.33
Is committed to implementing the organization's vision on a day-to-day basis	4	5	4
MANAGEMENT:	3.42	4.39	3.87
Business Operations:	3.2	3.83	3.17
Knows and understands the internal business operations	3	4	3
Demonstrates an understanding of how the organization is run	4	4	4
Is quick to respond when external business issues can impact the organization	4	4	3
Uses a knowledge of market and environmental trends when making decisions	3	4	4
Is quick to address difficult employee situations	2	4	2
Uses and communicates financial information to manage effectively	6	3	3
Plans:	3	5	3.88
Creates dialogue regarding goals and objectives with the group to ensure clarity	3	5	4
Considers time and resources required when establishing goals	4	5	4.5
Sets realistic estimates of human and physical resources needed when planning	3	5	4
Plans and organizes work in a systematic manner	2	5	3
Implements:	3.5	4.5	4
Gets things done through effective use of resources	3	5	4
Takes corrective actions and modifies plans to get the best results possible	4	5	3.67
Has the insight to see what needs to be done and does it	3	5	4.33
Maintains a commitment to meeting project goals in the face of obstacles	4	3	4
Project Management:	3.5	3.33	3.72
Adapts unique strategies to get things done	4	3	3.67
Sets clear and appropriate timelines to achieve project goals	3	3	4
Manages work processes effectively and efficiently	6	4	3.5
Time Management:	3	4.67	4.33

Survey Items	Self	Boss	Peers
Is concerned about getting things done on time	5	5	5
Insists that things get completed when they are promised	2	5	4.33
Has objectives which are time specific and measurable	2	4	3.67
Computer Literacy:	4.33	5	4.11
Has sufficient computer skills to function efficiently in the organization	4	5	4.33
Is proficient in computer applications appropriate to work responsibilities	4	5	4
Uses available computer resources to get the job done	5	5	4
INTERPERSONAL:	4.03	3.72	3.63
Manages Diversity:	5	4	4
Is able to work with others from diverse backgrounds	5	5	4.33
Creates an atmosphere of inclusiveness in the work environment	5	3	3.67
Manages Conflict	3.75	3.5	3.21
Anticipates and deals with problems before they become unmanageable	5	4	4
Is sensitive to internal dynamics of the organization	4	4	3.5
Works to quickly resolve conflicts by acting objectively and decisively	2	3	3
Shows confidence and composure when dealing with challenges and ambiguities	4	3	2.33
Establishes Networks:	3.33	3.67	3.67
Teams up well with internal and external people to get things done	3	5	4.33
Engages colleagues inside and outside the organization to exchange information	4	3	4
Networks internally and externally to seek advice and support	3	3	2.67
CONCEPTUAL:	3.97	4.33	3.69
Fosters Innovation:	3.67	3.25	3.29
Encourages the use of creative ideas of others in an effective manner	4	3	4
Looks for promising ideas and takes the necessary risks to try them	4	3	2.33
Generates new concepts and ideas that are not apparent to others	6	4	3.33
Creates unique and leading-edge ideas to enhance organizational performance	3	3	3.5
Analyzes Problems:	4.25	4.75	4.17
Studies all information about a problem and discerns what is important	5	5	4.67
Focuses on relevant details while keeping a big picture perspective	4	4	4.33
Is able to understand what is most important when dealing with complex issues	4	5	3.67
Draws sound conclusions by assessing relevant information	4	5	4
Evaluates Decision Options:	4	5	3.61
Strives to make balanced decisions even when there are competing priorities	4	5	4
Uses adequate information and alternative solutions to make sound decisions	4	5	3.33
Considers consequences of various options and chooses the best alternatives	4	5	3.5
COMMUNICATION:	4.04	4.13	3.68
Listens Actively:	5	4	3.16
Takes time to reflect upon what someone is saying before responding	5	4	3
Makes a conscious effort not to interrupt others	5	4	3.33
Writes Effectively:	4	5	3.72
Effectively and clearly presents ideas in written form	4	5	3.5
Concisely writes technical information in an understandable manner	6	5	3.67
Is able to present written information in understandable language	4	5	4
Speaks Effectively:	3.67	4.5	4
Uses clear and concise language when speaking	4	5	3.67
Presents ideas in a logical way where the point is clear when speaking	4	4	4.33
Prepares and presents effective speeches appropriate to the topic announced	3	6	4
Delivers Presentations:	3.5	3	3.84
Designs presentations that reach every level of understanding in the group	4	6	4
Effectively presents information in a natural manner	3	3	3.67
ORGANIZATIONAL STRATEGY:	3.88	4.11	3.75
Customer And Community Orientation:	4.67	4.67	4.33
Demonstrates an interest in receiving customers' input about products/services	5	5	4.67
Anticipates the effect of important decisions on internal and external customers	4	4	4
Strives to meet and exceed customers' expectations	5	5	4.33

Survey Items	Self	Boss	Peers
Organizational Performance Improvement:	3.5	4	3.42
Uses a systematic approach in planning, monitoring, and improving processes	2	4	2.5
Practices performance improvements methods in day-to-day work situations	6	4	3
Understands and applies performance improvement methods to achieve goals	6	3	3.5
Works to ensure seamless delivery of services to internal and external customers	5	5	4.67
Technology:	3.33	4	3.29
Stays informed about new technology developments in their field	4	4	4
Presents ideas about new technical information for use in the organization	3	6	2.5
Adopts new technology which can promote organizational performance	6	4	3.33
Demonstrates a working knowledge of current technology and applications	3	4	3.33
Occupational Technical Knowledge:	4	3.75	3.96
Maintains a high level of competency in occupational technical areas of his/her job	4	5	3.67
Is thoroughly familiar with new industry developments, policies, and practices	3	3	3.67
Shows a high level of expertise in their technical area	6	4	4
Researches technical information about ideas and practices in their field	5	3	4.5

INDEX

Note: Additional display material is indicated in **bold**.

ABOUT THE AUTHOR

Peter A. Topping, Ph.D., is a senior lecturer and executive director of executive education at Goizueta Business School at Emory University, ranked by *BusinessWeek* as having one of the country's leading executive MBA programs. Dr. Topping's work has appeared in several professional publications, including *Business and Economics Review* and *Journal of World Business*. He has worked with a broad range of global organizations, including Coca-Cola, Bosch, Unum, Xerox, and Eastman Chemical.